Spiritual Renaissance

Spiritual Renaissance

Elevating Your Consciousness for the Common Good

Barbara Condron

D.M., D.D., B.J.

SOM Publishing
Windyville, Missouri 65783 U.S.A.

By the same author

First Opinion: Wholistic Health Care in the 21st Century

The Work of the Soul

The Dreamer's Dictionary

Uncommon Knowledge

Kundalini Rising

What Will I Do Tomorrow?

Cover Art by Dr. Barbara Condron
Cover Design by Dan Salmo & Matthew Marian

ISBN: 0-944386-22-9

Library of Congress Catalogue Number pending

PRINTED IN THE UNITED STATES OF AMERICA

If you desire to learn more about the research and teachings in this book, write to School of Metaphysics, World Headquarters, Windyville, Missouri 65783.
Or call us at 417-345-8411.
Visit us on the Internet at www.som.org

"A human being is part of the whole, called by us 'universe', limited in time and space. He experiences himself, his thoughts and feelings as something separated from the rest – a kind of optical delusion of his consciousness. This delusion is a prison, restricting us to our personal desires and to affection for a few persons close to us.

Our task must be to free ourselves from our prison by widening our circle of compassion to embrace all humanity and the whole of nature in its beauty."

–Albert Einstein, German scientist (1879-1955)

The Contents

The Spiritual Renaissance

Interconnectedness

Freedom

Quickening

Birth

Awakening

Initiation

Awareness

Transformation

Quest

Destiny

Communion

Fulfillment

Interconnectedness

First thoughts...

As we experience the transition of one century to another, indeed one millennium to the next, we are also witness to a global transformation of consciousness.

Religious leaders note this change by how man reacts to what God, or the Universe, creates. From the aurora Borealis to miraculous healing, from common origins to earthquakes and tidal waves, religion begins by admitting and accepting the mysteries of the universe in humbled awe. Religion is the epitome of faith in a Creator greater than ourselves. It is the underpinning of all that will come. The ideas that birthed every religion that has ever existed on this planet reflect the early stages of man's reasoning, for in order for man to experience, he must first believe.

Scientists note this change by how the universe reacts to what man creates. From space probes seeking intelligent life in the universe to genetic manipulations, from the information highway to the garbage of a wasteful people, science begins by identifying and sometimes creating problems that it can then go about solving. Science is the epitome of man as creator. Rearranging his universe in his own image and likeness, humanity in general is experiencing the need to grow up, to replace awkwardness with grace, selfishness with benevolence. Now that man can believe, he must wield his powers of imagination, memory, and will for the common good.

The global transformation of consciousness that is upon us is the maturing of reasoning and the birthing of intuition, individually and collectively.

What until now, for most, has been instinct can evolve with understanding. We can move beyond believing in our instinct – be it the impulse that fuels the artist or the drive that makes the statesman or the urge that forms a parent – never asking where it comes from or how long it will stay. Such is the limitation of religion as we have known it until now. We can expand our consciousness to go beyond what we physically experience with the bodily senses – what we hear with our ears or calculate based upon what we see with our eyes – the limitations of science up to now.

Now we can forge a new consciousness. We can move into a new phase of understanding by using what has been gained through religion and through science from the past millennia. We can evolve as a species from Reasoning Man to Intuitive Man, the completion of a cycle of consciousness. Astrologers note this change as the movement from the age of Pisces, the believer, into the age of Aquarius, the knower. I and other metaphysicians describe this period as the evolvement of root races, significant levels of existence that are present within our ever-changing universe. As the most evolved life form on our planet, humanity's consciousness is about to manifest a destiny foretold by prophets, oracles, and statisticians worldwide for millennia – Spiritual Man.

Spiritual Renaissance is at once a history of where we have come from, a perspective of where we are, and a prophetic vision of where we are going. The ideas described here are timeless.

The subject matter of each chapter is illustrated in two ways. First they are explored in narratives drawing largely upon addresses given from 1984 through 1999. It is my hope that my love of Universal Truth shines forth in the choice of memorable quotations from some of the most visionary people who have walked on this earth. I also trust my willingness to be forthright and forthcoming concerning how my own life has unfolded will resonate within your own being, and in that way elevate your spirit.

Following each narrative you will find an essay. I like to think these are my tribute to some of the authors I have admired all my life, people like Ralph Waldo Emerson, William Shakespeare and Helen Keller. Like writers such as these, I have attempted to capture the reality of our times for what it reveals about our universal nature. Each essay is a companion piece to what has come before. It begins with a current event of the time, extracting a common lesson that illuminates who we are, and arrives at a new way of seeing who we can become.

It is a wonderful time to be experiencing in the physical, material plane of existence. It is an optimal time to commune with your Creator and realize your relationship to and with all of creation. It is the perfect time to accelerate your own and humanity's evolution. For now is the time you possess.

Now is a time ripe with opportunity, responsibility, and Enlightenment.

A time of Spiritual Renaissance.

May peace be with you all ways.

Dr. Barbara Condron

"The time draws near the birth of Christ;
The moon is hid, the night is still;
A single church below the hill
Is pealing, folded in the mist.

A single peal of bells below,
That wakens at this hour of rest
A single murmur in the breast,
That these are not the bells I know.

Like strangers' voices here they sound,
In lands where not a memory strays,
Nor landmark breathes of other days,
But all is new unhallowed ground.

Ring out, wild bells, to the wild sky,
The flying cloud, the frosty light:
The year is dying in the night;
Ring out, wild bells, and let him die.

Ring out the old, ring in the new,
Ring, happy bells, across the snow:
The year is going, let him go;
Ring out the false, ring in the true.

Ring out the grief that saps the mind,
For those that here we see no more;
Ring out the feud of rich and poor,
Ring in redress to all mankind.

Ring out a slowly dying cause,
And ancient forms of party strife;
Ring in the nobler modes of life,
With sweeter manners, purer laws.

Ring out the want, the care, the sin,
The Faithless coldness of the times;
Ring out, ring out my mournful rhymes,
But ring the fuller minstrel in.

Ring out false pride in place and blood,
The civic slander and the spite;
Ring in the love of truth and right,
Ring in the common love of good.

Ring out old shapes of foul disease;
ring out the narrowing lust of gold;
Ring out the thousand wars of old,
Ring in the thousand years of peace.

Ring in the valiant man and free,
The larger heart, the kindlier hand;
Ring out the darkness of the land,
Ring in the Christ that is to be."

- by Alfred, Lord Tennyson
In Memorium

I

The Spiritual Renaissance

Interconnectedness

"*No man is an island, entire of itself;*
every man is a piece of the continent,
a part of the main.
If a clod be washed away by the sea,
Europe is the less, as well as if a promontory were,
as well as if a manor of thy friend's or of thine own were.
Any man's death diminishes me
because I am involved in mankind;
and therefore never send to know for whom the bell tolls;
it tolls for thee."

– English poet and divine John Donne (1572-1631)

Spiritual Renaissance
A Stream of Consciousness

When you toss a stone into a still pool, the water ripples out in a series of widening circles.

Conjure this image in your mind's eye. Ask yourself how one ripple affects another, and where does the energy of the ripples go? Why are you able to create images in your mind, seemingly out of nothing?

What enables us to see pictures that exist only in response to our beckoning is an inherent capacity for genius. It is a divine, and universal, urge to create described in classical and Holy works for centuries. The skill to ask the right questions – the hows and wheres and whys – sets us on the path of Self mastery.

With this stream of consciousness you open your mind to interconnectedness. Interconnectedness is reflective of both the need and the fulfillment of the self and the other, the individual and the all, the microcosm and the macrocosm. The energies available to us are quite fitting as we prepare to close one century, one millennium, and open another.

You probably know more about interconnectedness than you have considered. Our present day existence lends itself well to it. From telephones that immediately link us to people we cannot see or touch to foods grown on another continent that appear on our dinner table to the immediate impact of a distant ruler's decision, the world has become a very small place.

As a child I was taught how to imagine a Creative Source of all Being. This Source I learned to call God. The sentiment in the childhood song: *"Jesus loves the little children all the children of the world. Red and yellow, black and white, they are precious in his sight. Jesus loves the little children of the world"* was impressed upon my consciousness from birth, laying the foundation for a true sense of brotherhood through my adult years. Interconnectedness. I learned early that we might have different earthly parents but we all come from the same Spiritual Parent.

I would move through life seeking to understand what connects us all. My desire to know what "makes people tick", as I learned to intellectually explain it in high school and college, drew people seeking counsel to me like a magnet. I tried as best I knew how to look beyond appearances for what was inside a person. In this way the early spiritual training was always with me, even when I might rebel against it, disconnecting myself in what I wholeheartedly believed was an effort to understand me.

The yearning to know self was much stronger than any egoic discord, any rationalization that erected barriers between me and others. That yearning was an attractive nucleus bringing others into my life and me into theirs in transforming ways. This became clear to me only because I chose to study at the School of Metaphysics.

School of Metaphysics lessons and disciplines elevated my sense of connectedness. Here I learned how to dispel the self-created barriers and unite my own consciousness. I learned what it means that each of us, every person, is like a pebble on the beach. I learned I am not the beach, but I am a part of the beach. And when one pebble is gone it is missed. Interconnectedness.

With metaphysical education, I experienced meditation as the answer to my prayer, coming to know that a sense of God's presence is essential to my well-being, and how communion with Him is spiritual fulfillment. Teaching others is a natural response for me, for it is the means by which I am able to give others the opportunities someone was willing to give to me.

Through teaching, I came to understand the cause of combination and connection, both elements of the principles of interconnectedness. Increasingly, I realized the study of Universal Law applies to all humans, all life forms, all substance and energy in our universe. On Mars and Pluto as well as on Earth, in the sea as well as on the land, Universal Law is ever present. Omnipresent. It is what makes us interconnected.

For more than a decade I traveled throughout the Midwest, teaching, lecturing, and serving in one capacity or another in the School of Metaphysics. In large part what motivated me to get out of bed, get in my car, and drive 100-500 miles almost every day was subconscious sensitivity to the needs of others. When approaching each city, the cries for help multiplied, becoming louder, and I wanted to ease people's pain by teaching them how to live a better life.

Teaching is a means to fulfill the Law, for it connects us to ourselves and to each other. *"He who aids others to abundance finds himself abundant."* Through the years, I have established connections with people that transcend time and space. The School of Metaphysics has provided me the opportunity to realize these bonds of divine love extend far beyond the present life experience.

Teaching is the connectedness of learning. They are inseparable. "*You cannot cast your bread upon the waters*" without it returning to you. And so it is with all pairs of opposites. They are interconnected in the consciousness of the Enlightened.

Years ago a teacher introduced me to a man who has become very important in my life, particularly of recent times for obvious reasons. He is a man I have held in awe and high esteem, someone worthy of study and emulation. He is known as the definitive representative of the Italian Renaissance - Leonardo da Vinci.

Da Vinci explored connectedness in his work. He called it

connessione. Five hundred years before the rest of humanity, he proposed its reality by noting, *"The earth is moved from its position by the weight of a tiny bird resting upon it."* Like a Zen master, he saw connectedness in nature, *"Mountains are made by the currents of rivers. Mountains are destroyed by the currents of rivers."* He demonstrated it by dissecting bodies, understanding the human body as a whole system, *"putting before your eyes a description of the whole form and substance of man."* Indeed it is his command of connectedness that endowed his most famous work, the Mona Lisa, with her timelessness. She is da Vinci's supreme statement of the principle of yin and yang. Interconnectedness.

In 1980 physicist David Bohm - the father of the theory of the holographic universe which posits that the genetic code of the universe is held in every atom just as a strand of DNA holds the entire genetic code of an individual - wrote, *"Everything is enfolded into everything."* Five centuries earlier Leonardo, without advantage of all that has revealed itself in that time, came to the same conclusion: *"Everything comes from everything, and everything is made out of everything, and everything returns into everything."*

Being a student and teacher of human potential has led me to visionary conclusions about the inherent nature in human beings, individually and collectively. Understanding the structure of consciousness lends great insight into the whys that puzzle most.

I believe the Italian Renaissance was a prophetic glimpse of what is to come.

I believe the present is the time of fulfillment of that prophecy.

The Italian Renaissance paved the way for genius to express itself in all avenues valued by Mankind – logical-mathematical, verbal-linguistic, artistic discipline, scientific curiosity, social-governmental, intrapersonal-educational. Over the past five hundred years, individuals around the planet have manifested the prophecy.

The list is impressive: Isaac Newton, Marie Curie, Benjamin Franklin, Thomas Jefferson, William Shakespeare, Michelangelo, Georgia O'Keeffe, Emmanuel Swedenborg, Buckminster Fuller, Amadeus Mozart, Ella Fitzgerald, F. M. Alexander, Muhammad Ali, Nelson Mandela, Mahatma Gandhi, Queen Elizabeth I, Albert Schweitzer, Thich Nhat Hanh, Mother Teresa, Rudolph Steiner, Maria Montessori. Though not all contemporaries, they had much in common. Most outstanding: *the willingness to elevate their consciousness for the common good.* The whole has been increased because these ones are part of it. We are better because they existed.

Now begins the time of moving beyond isolated manifestations of genius. No more will countries claim a single genius in one area of endeavor then wait centuries for another to arise.

Within recent centuries we have seen increasing manifestations of simultaneous genius; da Vinci and Michelangelo, William Shakespeare and Sir Francis Bacon, Thomas Edison and Nicola Tesla. Now is the time to cultivate personal excellence, to come away from the entrapment of materialistic thinking and turn our minds to the essence of life where meaning resides. Firmly seated within this consciousness, this interconnectedness, we can hope to answer any question, to resolve any problem.

We will embody a renaissance of the spirit the like of which Mankind has yet to witness. The reality of interconnectedness can spread like a wave through each human being, cleansing mind and body and uplifting the spirit.

The ever-expanding circle in the pool is the principle of Interconnectedness. Life, existence, is the pool. Evolution is the widening circles emanating from the center, the beginning. The stone is what can be.

The question is: Who will toss the stone?

"The first day or so
we all pointed to our countries.
The third or fourth day
we were pointing to our continents.
By the fifth day
we were aware of only one Earth."

—Discovery 5 Space Mission

Living Peaceably begins by Thinking Peacefully

an essay first published in November 1996

The simplicity of these few words continues to resound throughout my being. They so readily convey the expansion of man's consciousness, the movement from ego-centered possessiveness to Spirit-centered unity.

It is easy to imagine that when your point of reference is no longer *on* Earth, your attachment *to* Earth and earthly things changes.

Many astronauts have commented on the miracle of actually seeing the planet revolving in space, as if it were a celestial child's radiant top spinning in thin air. This view is divergent with the commonly-accepted state of mind shared by most humans. Too many people see others as strangers rather than spiritual brothers and sisters. Too many remain more concerned about their own welfare than the good of all concerned. Too many allow their own egos to blind their perception of the joy, wonder, and Truth that exists in all nations, all cultures, all creeds. Too many falsely believe to listen to another's point of view is to, in some way, defile or abandon your own. And too many are willing to die for those beliefs, and to kill those who do not share them.

The common consciousness of mankind perpetuates the loneliness of the stranger, the selfishness of the greedy, the cruelty of the arrogant, the stubbornness of the closeminded, and the judgement of the murderer. Why? It seems these have been the prevailing thoughts of man since the beginning of time, why don't we learn? How can we transcend our own weaknesses and elevate the consciousness of mankind to a new benevolence?

Buddhism teaches that the source of all misery is attachment to the physical. The *Bible* and the *Koran* teach that sorrow occurs when you are separated or away from the presence of God. Where there is misery there is no peace. In every culture of the world there is still a hope for peace.

This *uncommon* consciousness arises above the sea of humanity like the astronauts whirling above the Earth. All great masters have displayed this transcendent consciousness without benefit of leaving the Earth. Each has pointed the way to a better way to think, a better way to live — a way more enlightened, more holy, more God-like. From the teachings of each great master spring what the world now knows as religion. Yet the Truth known and displayed by the few too often seems elusive or even absent in current religious climates. Every Christian knows the difference between a Sunday church-goer and a minister or priest. Every historian knows that more wars, the greatest inhumanities, have been conducted in the name of the Creator than in the name of science or progress. War is the reflection of man's own inner turmoil magnified, the result of the failures in the common consciousness.

For change to occur we must be willing to think new thoughts, to behave in new ways, to initiate new understandings. We must believe that we can transform the common into the uncommon. We must revive the essence of religion; its spiritual Truths. In its exalted form, religion is the expression of man's spiritual consciousness to the degree he is willing to commit himself to the divine pursuit of Godliness. For it to be real to you, your religion – your concept of God and the Truth – must touch your everyday life. It must be courted through daily meditation. It must motivate you and guide your every thought. It must reverberate throughout your being, dissipating any limitation to your peace of mind.

To know peace, we must be willing to see the uncommon in the common. In the midst of the current problems arising from man's attachments, we must learn to make peace with ourselves and each other. A great peacemaker of the 20th century, Mohandas Gandhi, said *"Each one has to find his peace from within. And peace to be real must be unaffected by outside circumstances."* At first it may seem impossible to find peace, and once discovered, difficult to keep, but the effort itself bears the understanding that will produce permanence.

"Undisturbed peace of mind is attained by the cultivation of friendliness toward the happy, compassion for the unhappy, delight in the virtuous, and indifference in the evil," counseled the Hindu teacher Patanjali over 2500 years ago. His advice is just as timely today.

We can make a difference in our own lives and in the lives of others. Living peaceably *does* begin by thinking peacefully. Join others in a synchronized effort to bring peace to our world during the noon hour Greenwich Mean Time on January first each year. Dedicate this hour to that which brings you peace of mind. Meditate. Walk in the woods. Pray with your family. Listen to your favorite symphony. Talk with a loved one. Read a fine book. As we spread this *Universal Hour of Peace* across the face of our planet, we can all come to know that we are of one Earth.

II

The Spiritual Renaissance

Freedom

"Freedom
(or this principle of freedom)
is the greatest gift conferred by God
on human nature; for through it
we have our felicity here as men,
through it
we have our felicity elsewhere as deities.

– Alighieri Dante, Italian poet (1265-1321)

Spiritual Renaissance

A Sea of Enlightened Faces

It is a special time to be alive.

Anyone incarned in the United States during the past 100 years has been witness to the most rapid advancement of Mankind's potential ever known. The outer physical advancements are the most apparent. We entered the century on horses and trains and we exit it in sports utility vehicles and space shuttles. We began with assembly line factories and local general stores and end with service jobs at home or in chain restaurants, department stores, and even auto parts stores. We began with one room schoolhouses and end with the global brain that is the internet's information superhighway.

Progress. In a deeper sense these reflect the quickening of genius that responds to need, inventiveness applied to the good of the whole.

Deeper still is the sense that Humanity – all homo sapiens, all males and females on this planet – has accelerated its collective soul progression in remarkable ways.

Consider what has transpired since 1900. Technology has brought us all together in ways most of us never imagined. Now, it is as if we all live in the same town, one "global village" as some describe it. What affects one, affects us all.

The philosophers among us say this has always been true for it is a Truth of our universe. We are interconnected. Knowledge of the world we live in reveals evidence of this connectedness with one another. The cure for disease *and* the spread of it, can circle the globe in a matter of hours. Possible nuclear fallout over Korea or Pakistan will in time affect the atmosphere over Chile and the United States. The strength of family is the cradle of civilization and the disintegration of it, the fall, now as in the past.

In the span of one hundred years we can see the workings of the laws of our universe, of cause and effect, karma if you will, on a worldwide scale. For instance, in 1900, Shintoism was reinstated in Japan against Buddhists' influences. By the end of the century, the 14th Dalai Lama remains in exile from Chinese-occupied Tibet. In a religiously diverse sense, the first Parliament of the World's Religions in 1893 is a small gathering of men, primarily from the U.S. and India; the centennial gathering in this century sees men and women from all religions of the world uniting in the same place with the intent to educate one another about their faiths. The International Church of Metaphysics finds its mission crystallized at this 1993 gathering. A name change reflects the transformation of identity the concept undergoes. While most of the world's religions remain self-consumed, a few are beginning to exchange ideas. These ones are trying to listen to one another, even building friendships. Into this arena of separatism, the *Interfaith* Church of Metaphysics exists to unite the individual and all of humanity in a quest of spiritual progression by drawing upon the truths that are universal, truths that are described in *every* Holy scripture the world has ever known.

1900 sees the first trial flight of the Zeppelin while 1998 sees one of mankind's first space travelers return to space at the age of 70 for another celestial trip while others live for years circling the Earth in the spaceship Mir (peace). Airplane travel is as commonplace as bus trips were in 1950 United States. Our capacity to quickly transport ourselves from one physical location to another introduces us to different people and their cultures, thus broadening our understanding of ourselves. Astral travel - from intuitive diagnosis to near death experiences to mind-to-mind contact over thousands of miles of physical distance - spoken of by the great masters of spirit is now a subject capturing public imagination as we stand on the threshold of the new millennium.

In 1900, Austrian psychoanalyist Sigmund Freud's *Interpretation of Dreams* is published to his contemporaries' scorn. Freud dares to bring what has been unconscious, evenly collectively so, into the light of day. He boldly asks the question every self-aware person will someday ask, "Why?" Throughout the century, the search for the meaning of our dreams will dovetail with man's greatest pursuit – understanding himself and his neighbor. In the coming years self study, self examination, self realization, and self determination will blossom, often conflicting with contemporary religious and scientific thought. Swiss psychiatrist Carl Jung will build upon Freud's work, investigating archetypes, universal symbology. Three-fourths of the way into the century the School of Metaphysics will embark upon dream research that will see the fruition of what Freud began.

By mid-century J. B. Rhine's *New World of the Mind* and Martin Heidegger's *Introduction to Metaphysics* are opening new lines of thinking. By the '70's, meditation comes to America in the form of Transcendental Meditation founder Maharishi Yogi and nothing will ever be the same again. People are beginning to talk about themselves. The School of Metaphysics begins openly teaching the development of consciousness to people of all ages, from all walks of life, all religious and educational backgrounds in 1973. No longer must one leave the world in order to cultivate spiritual enlightenment. By the end of the century, words like visualization, intuition, and spirituality are "mainstream" and everyone wants to know the meaning of his or her dreams!

In 1900, Max Planck's formulation of the quantum theory begins the journey that will lead to understanding the building blocks of life, the discovery of DNA and genetic science which produces animal clones in several places on the planet. Beyond man's reaching to be like his Creator, is the outstanding advancement that will lead science and religion to intersect, that will place *meta* with the word *physics* in more people's minds.

In 1900, American scientist R. A. Fessenden transmits human speech via radio waves beginning a quick ascension to the intricate mass communication network that connects everyone on the planet by the end of the century. A physical means of telepathy and teleportation. A world of virtual reality that will challenge us to determine the value of information and experience to ourselves and our posterity. A challenge that will fuel the desire to move beyond believing to fulfill the need to know.

The signs of transformation are everywhere.

Consider this. What average Americans did for themselves in 1900, we pay others to do for us in 1999. Raising, preserving, and even preparing food. Building houses. Caring for and educating our children. Even cleaning our clothes, houses, and offices. Technology has eased many "burdens", freeing us to have time to do those things we always said we wanted to do.

In the U.S. at the close of the century, almost every household owns at least one car, at least one phone, and at least one television. Almost half have some type of computer.

What is more startling is to hold this in mind while considering a bit of hypothetical mathematics. The hypothesis goes like this.

If we could shrink the entire population of the world to a village of precisely 100 people, with all existing human ratios remaining the same, the composition would be as follows:

There would be 57 Asians, 21 Europeans, 14 from North and South America, and eight Africans.

51 would be female; 49 would be male.

70 would be nonwhite; 30 would be white.

70 would be non-Christian; 30 would be Christian.

50% of the entire world's wealth would be in the hands of only six people and all six would be citizens of the United States.

80 would live in substandard housing.

70 would be unable to read.

50 would suffer from malnutrition.

1 would be near death; 1 would be near giving birth.

Only 1 would have a college education.

No one would own a computer yet.

This puts our incredible wealth into perspective. People in the United States are so very fortunate to live in the one place on the planet where personal freedom and responsibility foster and promote personal excellence and visionary thinking. Our greatest challenge may be the continual investment of talented resources applied for the goodness of all. After all, the alternative is maintenance of, or worse depletion of, our inheritance.

Living in this country, at this time, demands the kind of thinking that is progressive, going beyond accepted limits. It demands imagination, as well as memory and the will power to employ good ideas. It demands the power available to all people, the power of reasoning.

There are times when technology presents us with happenings that cause us to wonder about others, and even ourselves. You know what they are: the murders, the thievery, the adultery, the dark side of mankind. Those profiting from harming others. The picture often painted by media is indeed impressionistic, and it is the opinion of its creator. Often ruled by another challenge to our wealth: unconscionable greed. In this case greed distorts the truth appealing to the baser, animal instincts in man. This too will in time pass.

Above all else the United States' good fortune can be attributed to the desire for and the willingness to change. It is the melding of desire and will that allows and encourages the progress that the world admires and emulates.

One of the brightest points in our technological future will be the increasing employment of it to enlighten consciousness – for visionary education that addresses the whole of Man and all of Mankind.

As it has made our lives physically easier, technology has challenged any limits in our consciousness. It has opened the world. It has given us humanity in our homes. In reality, very few people are like us when the only way we know to identify and experience is with the outer senses. The inner senses bring awareness of interconnectedness. Now, in large part because of the wealth technology has brought us, we must cultivate those inner senses to transcend our limitations.

We must remember where we have come from so we can respond in wisdom to those who are reaching up to us for help.

We must imagine where we can go so we in turn reach up for the guidance of those who have come before us.

We must learn how to look beyond the color of skin or sound of a voice, ceasing to be deceived by appearances. We must look for what unites us *without being distracted by our differences*.

In this way we can hope to learn how to live the tenets described in every Holy Scripture in the world. Whether tens of millennia ago or a mere century, Truths that apply to us all are universal, existing beyond the time and the space of physical existence. Every individual who has embraced a religious concept has learned the Truth that so well embodies the Principle of Interconnectedness. It is what is commonly called *The Golden Rule*:

> *"All things whatsoever ye would that men should do to you, do ye even so to them."*
> *- Matthew 7:12, Bible, Christianity*

> *"This is the sum of duty: do naught unto others which would cause you pain if done to you."*
> *- Mahabarata 5:1517, Hinduism*

> *"No one of you is a believer until he desires for his brother that which he desires for himself."*
> *- Sunnab, Islam*

> *"What is hateful to you, do not to your fellow man. That is the entire Law; all the rest is commentary."*
> - *Torah,* Judaism

> *"In happiness and suffering, in joy and grief, regard all creatures as you would regard your own self."*
> *- Lord Mahavir 24th Tirthankara, Jainism*

"Hurt not others in ways that you yourself would find hurtful." - Dhammapada, Buddhism

"Respect for all life is the foundation"
- The Great Law of Peace, Native American Indian

"Be not estranged from another for God dwells in every heart." - Gura Granth Sahib, Sikkism

"Blessed is he who prefers his brother before himself."
- Baha'u'llah, Baha'i Faith

"Regard your neighbor's gain as your own gain, and your neighbor's loss as your own loss."
- Tai Shang Kan Ying Pi'en, Taoism

"That nature only is good when it shall not do unto another whatever is not good for its own self." - Dadistan-i-Dinik, 94:5, Zoastrianism

We cannot be forced to love one another. The reasoning mind says we must accept love's place in our lives. Not to avoid things undesired or feared, nor to foster a false sense of security or self-importance, rather we must bring love into our lives. Love is the one incentive capable of transforming compulsive, animal man into intuitive, spiritual man. Sooner or later, every individual will be a channel for love. Each will come to embody love in the ways taught by the Buddha, and by the Christ, for love is our true essence and light is our capacity to realize it.

We must learn to love one another because now, at last, we can. We are ready. We are capable of understanding what unites us as a people - the common origin, the common experience, the common destiny.

It would have made a difference in my life had I learned as a child that such Truths are universal. Who might I now be had I been raised from birth with the knowledge that all people are taught similar codes of humanity? What sense of interconnectedness might I experience now? Some may describe the Truth more eloquently than another, but the essence of the Truth remains and is the same. How empowering to learn of the common ground we share with others around the world.

How enlightening to make that Truth a part of the fibre of your being, a part of your thinking so fervently embraced and understood that no man is ever a stranger to you! Technology can accelerate our growth for it brings the men and women of the world to our doorstep. Everyday our physical realm of experience is broadened through television and radio, subliminally demanding an expansion of our consciousness.

We have come so far since the early days of animalistic man, what historically is remembered as less civilized beings. Our collective consciousness has grown since the days of Atlantis, the days symbolized by the *Bible*'s King David and the *Mahabarata*'s Arjuna. Cro-Magnon man realized he could move upright and wield tools with independent juxtapositioning of fingers thus broadening man's experience. This was the impetus forging the evolutionary development of a larger forebrain for storing records of experience.

What followed was remarkable, forever separating man from all other animals on earth. Now man possessed the tools to build the faculty of memory. This was a physical renaissance in mankind's quest to be like his Maker.

This physical renaissance has been dominant for a quarter million years. The capacity to remember is essential for man to move beyond animal instinct. It is also essential in the development of reasoning. The invention of reasoning characterizes the evolutionary development of the human being.

For millennia, our species has aspired to combine memory, will and the most recent development – imagination. Man's proclivity for thinking has produced breathtaking works: the Sistine Chapel painting, Hoover Dam, space probes throughout our universe, the Panama Canal, and sonatas by Bach and Beethoven and Brahms. History has seen enough man-made wonders to record the finest.

Δ the *Great Pyramid of Khufu* (Cheops) at Giza is the only one of the Seven Wonders of the World still standing. Estimated time of building 2500 BC.

Δ the *Hanging Gardens of Babylon* built on the banks of the Euphrates by Nebuchadnezzar II as a gift to his wife around 600 BC.

Δ the *Statue of Zeus* at Olympia near Athens celebrated the patron of the Olympic games. Sculpted 440 BC.

Δ the *Temple of Artemis* at Ephesus (Turkey) said to have been the most beautiful structure on earth was built 550 BC and destroyed in 401.

Δ the *Mausoleum at Halicarnassus* (SW Turkey) was a gigantic, 140 foot high tomb was completed in 350 BC for a Persian satrap (governor). It was dismantled in 1494.

Δ the *Colossus at Rhodes* was a 110 foot statue of the Greek sun god Helios symbolized peace and freedom. Completed in 282 BC, an earthquake toppled it in 226 BC where it remained until Arab invaders dismantled it in 654.

Δ the *Pharos of Alexandria*, the 40-story lighthouse in the harbor of then Egyptian capital Alexandria was for centuries the tallest building on earth. Completed around 300 BC, earthquakes damaged this wonder until in 1480 an Egyptian sultan took the marble from the lighthouse to build a fort for Alexandria's defense.

In time the wonders of the ancient world gave way to candidates of the Middle Ages, nominees from a wider world view: *Temples in Aswan* (Egypt) and *Angkor Wat* (Cambodia), the *Giant Monoliths of Rapa Nui* (Easter Island), the *Taj Mahal* (India), the *Leaning Tower of Pisa* (Italy), the *Great Wall of China*, *Gate of All Nations* (Iran), and perhaps *Stonehenge* (England), *Colosseum of Rome*, and *Machu Picchu* (Peru) should be considered. The impact is awesome, for these reflect a world of human beings growing and developing. Humanity, wherever it is found on the globe, is experiencing an expansion of consciousness.

The creation of a new list of world wonders is also a testament to the transitory nature of our physical world. The ancient wonders have passed away. So it is with all things of the material world.

Life and death are the means for measuring linear time. The movement of the Earth on its axis and around the Sun, knowledge unknown just centuries ago and still not known by most people on Earth, gives us a means for measuring our experience. It is how the creator is transformed, the beauty and strength and permanence created within, that is eternal.

The manifestation of our desires in the physical world, be they pyramids or gardens, a new car or a marriage and family, are merely the point when we must *respond* to the acquisition. It is common knowledge that a car depreciates in value several thousand dollars the minute you drive it off the seller's lot. Only in the use of the car can we discover its true value to us, not in the mere ownership. Yet how many people are owned by their possessions? When this begins to occur, the physical renaissance has ended, and the next stage in evolution is past due.

As Shakespeare's Hamlet notes, *"There is nothing either good or bad but thinking makes it so."* The next renaissance will be one of spirit, one of thinking, one of wisdom.

Those who mate and make a life with another, are those who have made the transition from thinking physically to thinking mentally. They understand the wedding is the commencement of a new life, more than an end to the old one. Their eyes are on the future they will make together. Such couples are visionaries and their lives are a dream in the making. Their love, the people they become, will be their legacy, more than any amount of money or possessions.

Anyone who lives a good, full life knows this secret. Either consciously or unconsciously, they realize that the nature of the physical is change. How we adapt is crucial to our sense of well being and in large part a result of our capacity to love. Hope is essential, but hope alone no longer satisfies a reasoner who has lived many years, seen many things, and like Freud has asked, "Why?"

We stand on the threshold of a Spiritual Renaissance the like of which mankind has yet to experience. This renaissance has been millennia in the making.

The European Renaissance with its glimpse of mind-expanding thought and capability was but a foreshadow of what is to come. As its greatest master, Leonardo Da Vinci, said, *"The desire to know is natural to good men."* The coming Spiritual Renaissance is the fruition of his insight.

Spiritual Renaissance is the movement in consciousness where knowing supersedes believing.

Where intuition is called upon in partnership with reasoning.

Where genius is promoted and mystical experience nurtured.

Where the consciousness of Mankind advances by choice, not by reaction.

Where the individual comes to realize his sole purpose for existence upon this plane, now or at any other time, is to become compatible to his Maker.

Then, at long last, the Buddha Consciousness, the Cosmic Consciousness, the Christ Consciousness will spread across the face of the Earth in a sea of Enlightened faces.

Perhaps that is another lesson in this change of consciousness that we are embarking upon. There are indeed absolutes. There are Universal Principles, Laws, Truths, that govern creation as we know it.

The Collective Consciousness

The Truth and Nothing But...

I was listening to an interview concerning audio tapes that American President Lyndon Johnson had recorded in the 1960's. An excerpt was being played where the President was being informed that a high-ranking member of his government had just been arrested for sexual misconduct.

Johnson's response was composed, measured, and short. Few words, much detail, as I often tell my students.

A tape of a conversation between Johnson and his wife Lady Bird followed. Lady Bird was explaining to her husband what she intended to say to the press when asked about the situation. Her belief was that he was a good Catholic, he was married with six children, and this unfortunate event could be nothing more than a momentary nervous breakdown from the pressures he was facing.

After the airing of this recording the female interviewer said something that took me by surprise. Departing from the possibility of a thoughtful question or insightful commentary, she slipped into common vernacular saying, "You go, Lady Bird." The '90's slang – meant to show support, acceptance, and encouragement between people, particularly female to female – was so out of place. A modern anachronism.

It may seem odd, but at that moment, with those four words, a visionary perspective was revealed to me. All of a sudden all the pieces of the renaissance puzzle came together.

One of the harbingers of the European Renaissance was what was called the Black Death, the plague. This disease swept quickly across Europe, leaving fewer survivors than it claimed. It was devastating. Yet the effect of the plague was more than a leveling, a balancing of the population. The Black Death changed the consciousness of everyone. The disease was universally potent. It showed no favoritism. It struck young and old, rich and poor, peasant and titled, religious and secular. That reality transformed the consciousness of a people prone to believe without question that their station in life was in some way preordained, out of their control and unresponsive to their desire.

Five hundred years of thinking about free will has indeed changed the face of the earth. As we close one millennium and open the next the "black death" is returning, not as a disease of the body but as a dis-ease in the collective consciousness. The tool for its dissemination is not another life form such as a virus; it is something we ourselves have created – technology. I believe multimedia is serving a similar purpose in the U.S. and abroad as did the European plague 500 years ago.

Since the days of settling in front of a box that delivered pictures and sound from far off cities for four, eight, twelve hours a day to the readily accessible 24-hour Internet and virtual reality, the changes in just fifty years are profound on the consciousness of man. My grandfather used to talk about the things he had seen in his life, from the turn of the century well into the 1900's. Most of what he talked about were the physical innovations, the movements from an agrarian society to an industrial one to a technological one. He personally witnessed the train, the automobile, mass transportation, space travel.

Without doubt it was the communication devices – telephones, radios, and television – that affected collective consciousness the most. These brought two World Wars to our doorstep, as well as space travel and civil rights battles, Miss Americas and football games. They continue to shape who we are and how we live.

Communication devices affect individual and collective consciousness. The information superhighway enables all of us to live in the same city. The same "global village" as it's called. We all live in the same town and we know most of the people in it. Curiously, the virtual town relegates our leaders to being nothing more than the people next door, or at best the class president or town mayor. In this way, the ever-present media has provided humanity with a similar effect that the Black Death produced: leveling the playing field. In all the news events that have united us, from man landing on the moon to the disintegration of the Challenger minutes after take off, from the Scopes trial to the O.J. Simpson one, from President Kennedy's adultery or President Clinton's, media has let us know that generally speaking people are people.

We are beginning to share the making of history as a planet of sentient beings. Diana, Princess of Wales, was like the wealthy, privileged homecoming queen in the global town. We were invited to her wedding and greeted her newborns. Her untimely, early death shocked most people, and the whole town grieved her passing. Mother Teresa's passing was like losing the most committed service giver in the town, the religious elder who cared for the ailing babies from the wrong side of the tracks and would not let the more fortunate forget their presence. The Osama bin Ladens or the Timothy McVeighs of the world are like the town bullies or the leaders of gangs that threaten and terrorize the town. When given a chance to talk about the mayor's peccadilloes or a religious leader's visit to a nearby town, most would choose to gossip about the mayor.

This is exactly what happened in 1998 when network anchormen left Cuba where a Pope was visiting for the first time in decades to return to the States to cover a U.S. President's infidelity. Unfortunately, this is often the level of awareness in our media. The degree to which the media wants to control the line of talk in the town is the degree to which it caters to the darker nature in us all for it becomes ruled by the weakest in human nature. It was this seedier side of journalism that turned me away from pursuing a journalistic career.

Years ago I studied journalism at the oldest "j-school" in the world at the University of Missouri. My original motivation for this area of study was my desire to continue to learn throughout my life. I wanted to constantly meet new people and come to understand them. I wanted to find out why the little old man rides his bicycle down to the corner store every day at a certain time. I wanted to know who he is, what his life has been, what makes him do what he does. That burning desire led me to believe that journalism could be a field where I might fulfill this desire while providing a roof over my head and food on my plate.

Reality did not meet my expectations. Even in the early '70's journalism was beginning to become tainted with corporate greed. Ratings equal popularity equal financial backing was the journalistic equation. Truth took a backseat, or became twisted to mean getting the "goods" on someone. The muckraking, the looking for dirt, tabloid journalism it is called today, was not appealing to me.

Just as the black death was filled with consequences no one wanted to face, so much of what media reflects back to us, like a huge mirror in the town square, is unappealing and unattractive. It continually tells us of man's inhumanity to man, it is obsessed with disease and death, all the while steering clear of the area of our society that seeks to explain, understand, and resolve our pain; religion. In many ways journalism as we experience it is dispiriting and threatening to our very humanity.

Media is man's creation, a response to our desire to communicate, to share information and experience, with the largest audience possible. However nobly intended, the part of journalism that wants to *make* the news, change history in some way, is the part that has evolved into what we always called in my hometown plain, old gossip. Much of what we hear and see in mass media fails to rise above this level. Too often current dollar-driven news reporting seeks to entertain rather than inform, to excite or shock rather than educate and illuminate. Just imagine what will occur when this great nervous system of our planet, the multi-media communication system, begins giving us more accurate feedback of who we are!

At its best journalism enables us to see the commonalities in human behavior. It reveals that one person's actions are often like another, even midst differences in language or culture. It reports the affects of our actions, and sometimes unveils the truth. Somewhere beyond the intrusive probing of clumsy reporters – the "can you tell us how it feels to lose....your home, your job, your kids" mentality – exists a desire to understand ourselves, our own nature as human beings. Eventually this will lead to a recognition that it is the thought, the intention, behind the act that makes the difference. When this begins occurring the need for a new idealism will be born and the Spiritual Renaissance will come into being.

Media plays a big part in accelerating or retarding the progress of collective consciousness in this direction. The older Masters in the field say that great journalism does not dictate, it does not create the news. Great journalism reports the news, describing what is transpiring. It is meant to be objective, without personal prejudice of any kind. Those who honestly strive for this transcendent state of balance rise above trying to determine outcomes and provide the space for the listener and viewer to draw their own conclusions. Great journalism requires a spiritual mindfulness only beginning to make its appearance in the "you go, Lady Bird" mentality of media of today.

In an unconscious way and in spite of itself, media is ushering us into Spiritual Renaissance *because* it lacks objectivity. In this world, media seeks to polarize us. One analyst commenting on political opinion polls noted that during the time of the American Revolution – warring with Great Britain for the right to self-govern – one third of the people supported the war, one third were against it, and another third insisted it didn't matter. As far as public opinion goes, that kind of attitude hasn't really changed. It reflects the collective consciousness. It is also reflective of our country and, since the United States is composed of a melting pot of people who have come whether in this century or another from all over the planet, it can be said reflective of humankind. Take any issue, be it political, educational, moral, and you will have the same breakdown of opinion. People on one side, people on the opposing side, and people who are not so much in the middle as they are apathetic or too sparsely informed to know on what side they stand.

The underlying issue facing humanity as a whole

is being revealed through the lack of will power of the leader of the most powerful nation on Earth, the first elected United States president to be impeached for high crimes and misdemeanors. During his trial, for which he was acquitted of perjury and obstruction of justice charges, most television media repeatedly reduced the import of the cause of impeachment to the level of "lying about sex, everyone does it." The general attitude was "it can happen to anyone...he's one of us...give him a break!" It is interesting to note that many foreign countries have this same consciousness. "What's the problem?" they have said. I would have to say that the consciousness that produces that question *is* the problem.

The advent of the change of consciousness that is upon us is a transcending of these pairs of opposites not the denial or ignoring of them. This is not apathy. It is the objectivity every great journalist seeks. This is very much what many have envisioned for an evolutionary advanced mankind – a transcending to what the truth is, a discernment of what is universally important and applicable. What is in the best interest of us all. What is for the goodness of all concerned.

It is an interesting turn of events that is noteworthy. What is occurring in the United States at this time on our planet, as has been true since its founding over 200 years ago, is for the rest of the world a microcosm of what can be. Good. Bad. Indifferent.

For many years I have realized the importance of this country. Its government is revolutionary on the face of the Earth. The longevity of the republic is a benchmark for Earth. Our founding fathers were indeed visionaries that did strive to know universal principles, did struggle to apply them in their own lives, and did attempt to the best of their capabilities to create a government based upon those principles that would insure that a democratic republic could endure the test of time.

It is interesting that at this time in the life of that government, media would try to make our government, under the auspices of democracy, a popularity contest. But that is what happens when truth becomes a commodity to be bought or sold, the result of popular opinion or vote rather than an absolute, the reflection of principles that exist with or without us, before and after us. As experience grows in me, I have of late adopted the idea that a responsible media will accept no paid political advertisements and in its place be a forum for all candidates to meet and debate the issues. Often. This simple gesture would cure many governmental ills. It would shine the media spotlight on the individuals and what each represents, so the public at large can choose who best represents them.

The search to know truth must ultimately be independent of opinion. Impossible for a consciousness engrossed in the temporary nature of a physical world, possible only in the open mind of one willing to explore the connections existing in that which is beyond the material, physical world.

Universal Truth exists whether man does or not. Look to nature to find it. Beyond and before man's day as novice creator, truths of the universe existed. Those truths still do.

Understanding how those truths apply to man is what will move us from animal man to spiritual man. Truth is not a matter of public opinion or majority rule, not a function of governmental systems. Nor is it a function of religion, for truth exists whether you believe it or not.

What is truth? How much value do we put on it? How far away from truth have we come?

The concept of Christian forgiveness is far from passive. It requires repentance. Change. Not blind acceptance. Court decisions are often determined by circumstances, rather than Truth. That is not new in our justice system but perhaps in the light of a society becoming aware of Universal Law it is time for that system to change.

Perhaps that is another lesson in this change of consciousness that we are embarking upon. There are indeed absolutes. There are Universal Principles, Laws, Truths, that govern creation as we know it.

What life is truly about is our capacity, individually and collectively, to understand those principles, to harmonize with them, to be guided by them for our own maturing. So we may come to a point of wielding those principles with wisdom. How quickly we will progress when all of our communication springs from this intent.

Through the spirit and body of one person, Leonardo da Vinci gave us a glimpse of what can be. Truly the genius he displayed is present in us all, and now stirs seeking to awaken from its long dormant state.

We stand at the threshold of a spiritual renaissance. Foreshadowed by the European Renaissance centuries ago and only now reaching its fruition in a way that can affect significant numbers of people throughout the planet.

Only now can we have the whole picture fed back to us in flickering images and words of who we are. Only now can we see we are the same, no matter where we are on the earth, no matter who we are. Only now can we realize what those universals are, and that change in consciousness will bring us a renaissance of spirit the like of which no one has seen before.

III

The Spiritual Renaissance

Quickening

"The proverbs of all nations,
which are always the literature of reason,
are the statements of an absolute truth
without qualification.
Proverbs, like the sacred books of each nation,
are the sanctuary of intuitions.
That which the droning world,
chained to appearances
will not allow the realist to say in his own words,
it will suffer him to say in proverbs
without contradiction.
And this law of laws,
which the pulpit, the senate and the college deny,
is hourly preached in all markets and workshops
by flights of proverbs, whose teaching is as true
and as omnipresent as that of birds and flies."

- Ralph Waldo Emerson, American poet & essayist (1803-1882)

Spiritual Quickening
Pandora's Legacy to Man

Based upon an address by the same title first given in the summer of 1990.

I spent the first three cycles of my life in smaller towns, fifteen to thirty thousand people. They afforded a great advantage. I did not know everyone in the town, but having one public high school enabled me to come into contact with all my peers. It was a rich experience at a time when I was learning the shades of grey between black and white.

Thinking more would be better, I moved to progressively larger cities. College with 20,000 others in a town three times that size. Then Wichita, Kansas, with 150,000, later the million of New Orleans. A decade of criss-crossing the Midwestern U.S. from Dallas to Detroit to Denver enabled me to experience my largest city, Chicago. Millions of people in such a small space on the planet.

It was an adjustment to live in the quiet hamlet of Windyville, population 17.

The locals were not at all sure when the School of Metaphysics purchased 700 acres of land with the intention of building a college. Ten years had passed by the time I made Windyville my home, and the locals were still not sure about the School but they were starting to accept and even like the people.

Now as we draw closer to another decade of homesteading, most of the locals trust us.

It is a nourishing transformation, for me personally and for the work I share with many others.

Growing up, I never thought I'd live in the country. My dad will tell you my ruling passion as a teenager was to get out of "Dullsville", the name I had given the town we moved to when I was 12. I thought the country was too lonely and isolated. Had it come earlier in my life, before metaphysical studies, I probably would have missed its inherent gifts. One of these is the opportunity to experience creation in all of its forms.

There is fresh air, soothing to the lungs, energizing for the body. You can receive as much as you can possibly use. The land which embodies the College of Metaphysics campus enables one to become very intimate with minerals because we have a lot of rocks on this property. The plant life is lush, and we have each other as part of creation.

Nature puts us in contact with the reality of our existence. It reminds us of where we have come from and who we are. Nature lends itself to a type of experience that truly is magnificent as long as you use your senses wisely to produce experiences that will lead to deeper understandings of ourselves and each other.

Humanity's awareness of creation is quickening. It is quickening worldwide in a very physical way. Creation is more often a function of meeting the demand of temperamental spirits, immature in desire and experience. Creation is centered more upon what man wants to possess than how he can gain the wisdom he needs to wield the power he has.

The quickening is evident in the second thoughts of some influential people. For instance an increasing amount of thought is being devoted worldwide to preserving natural resources, to keeping our air and our water clean. Earth Day is a good example. A day set aside to think about how what we do affects the planet we inhabit. A time to seriously consider how the fulfillment of our physically-based desires affects the planet we inhabit. This is one response to *man's need to respect the planet* that he uses for his schoolroom.

Thought is cause, therefore this type of thinking will bear fruit as long as it is nourished. The real challenge to man as creator is his willingness to change, to let go of comfort in order to see his ideas fulfilled.

I'm reminded of a television commercial featuring a well-known actress talking about terrible, hideous things that are happening to animals. She implores you to call a 900 number and save those animals. She is talking about man's use of animals for experimentation for frivolous, self-seeking pursuits. Killing animals to make another perfume as opposed to risking an animal's life in place of a human volunteer – while testing a possible life-saving drug. This mindfulness is an attempt to *respect* the fact that *animals* are a part of creation, a part we would be served well to understand before we significantly alter the balance of nature.

Then there is our need to respect our own kind, *man's need to respect man.* Worldwide religious and political organizations try to feed the hungry and shelter the homeless. At their best, the former appeals to the heart of each individual for action, the latter to a unified, group consciousness with conscience. These activities are our response to attempt to respect one another, to respect humanity.

We can take this even farther.

Metaphysicians recognize the root of these concerns to be *man's need to know how to respond to his abilities as a creator.* At its essence this becomes an appreciation of where we've come from. By bringing spiritual evolutionary cycles, these "root races", into our collective conscious awareness we are better equipped to respond with wholistic thinking, and the genius it brings forth.

Science studies these root races by separating the disciplines; from anthropology to nuclear fission, from biological cloning to space exploration. Religious philosophy stimulates us to bring them all together, the wholeness of all creation. By uniting the disciplines an awareness of the need for us to cooperate with creation as it exists is born. We take a maturing step by responding to our creative potential. In this way we become visionary creators.

This is the importance of what might at times seem like pointless discussion. For instance the debate about cloning. Cloning animals and most probably humans is no longer science fiction, rather it is science fact. Only its accessibility is controlled for the moment. The time to debate whether we should or should not is long past.

The discussion now must be centered on how do we respond to man as creator? Cloning is a natural step in scientific evolution. Our challenge is to make it a natural step in our spiritual evolution.

Beyond the debate of who gets cloned and who doesn't, are more far reaching questions. In a world already brimming, do we risk overpopulation? If we do, in time will we risk retarding our evolutionary growth promoting weakness by ignoring survival of the fittest? Will we unintentionally open the world to plagues? Will we eventually become a race of a small group of people, either specialized to the point of extinction or generalized to the point of mediocrity?

At some point we will get past these kinds of hypothetical questions and hopefully settle our consciousness into the responsibility of our creative science. We will begin to prepare ourselves for what is now in our hands. We will begin to wonder how we can become the kind of being worthy of being cloned.

One of the most dreaded and potentially dangerous diseases of our time that infiltrates humanity is loneliness. When traveling into a large city it is easy to become sensitive and to hear loneliness. As the numbers of people multiply the desolation, the emptiness, can be overwhelming.

When you stop and think about it this is pretty amazing. Cities where thousands and millions of people congregate to live and work together could be meccas of spiritual community. The reality of bombs and guns, disease and illiteracy, leaves much desired. People do not become enriched in today's cities.

It is difficult to know life's richness without communion. For the most part people are isolated. They do not know the names of their neighbors, let alone their children's' teachers or community's leader. I do believe recognizing creation cures. Knowing your spiritual origin and your relationship with all people, heals. The ancient wisdom frees you to give freely, *"to love your neighbor as yourself."*

The ills of the world are many. Loneliness is only one of them. You can probably think of illnesses of a mental or spiritual variety in your own life. There is hatred. There is prejudice, and there is resentment. There is jealousy, and there is envy. There are all kinds of doubts and fears and manifestations of negative thinking.

The truth is for every ill there is a cure.

For every doubt there is the answer of faith fulfilled through reason.

For every fear there is an experience that brings enlightenment.

All the world's holy scriptures have attempted to identify the cause for this.

For the Jew and the Christian, the first book in the *Bible* tries to explain the cause for this illness by tracing it back to the man and the woman in the Garden of Eden. The serpent, the most cunning animal God created, tempts the woman to eat of the Tree of Knowledge of good and evil.

The Hindu scriptures, particularly the *Mahabarata*, trace it back to a battle between two warring tribes, the Kurus and the Pandus.

In Taoist scriptures, it is traced back to a separation from the *Tao*, or The Way, a path to reason.

In the Buddhist scriptures it is traced back to three sorrows which Prince Gautama defined at the age of 30 as disease and old age and death.

Perhaps the best illustration of what caused these illnesses to befall man appears in Greek Mythology. Greek Mythology is classical literature. It has endured because it is whole and complete as are all Holy Scriptures.

Greek mythology describes the creation of the world. Once the world was created there were Titans. The Titans were elder gods. Cronus, who is also known as Saturn, was the ruler of the elder gods. He sired many children. As his wife would birth them, he would swallow them, because he knew there was a destiny that one of his offspring would dethrone him someday.

His wife got smart after five kids and spirited away a male child who later became known as Zeus. This is reminiscent of Moses' story in Judeo-Christian traditions. Zeus was away for a time and he eventually came back and dethroned his father. Zeus, by the way is also known as Jupiter, for those who are interested in astrology. When Zeus took over he brought a Golden Age, a perfect time of peace and happiness.

It's at this point that a woman named Pandora shaped mankind's future.

For a long time only men were upon the earth. Zeus created women in his anger at Prometheus, a Titan involved in the creation of the world, for caring so much for men. Prometheus had not only stolen fire for men, he had also arranged that they should get the best part of any animal sacrificed and the gods the worst.

Prometheus butchered a great ox, and wrapped the good edible parts in the hide. He disguised them further by piling entrails on top. Beside this heap he put another of all the bones, dressed up with cunning and covered with shining fat and bade Zeus choose between them. Zeus took up the white fat and was angry when he saw the bones craftily arranged. But he had made his choice and had to abide by it.

Thereafter, only fat and bones were burned to the gods upon their altars. Men kept the good meat for themselves.

Zeus, the Father of Men and of Gods, swore revenge on mankind first, then on mankind's friend. He made a great evil for men in the likeness of a shy maiden. She was a sweet and lovely thing to look upon. Each of the twelve gods gave her gifts – silvery array and an embroidered veil, bright garlands of blooming flowers and a crown of gold – great beauty shown from it. Because of what they gave her, they called her Pandora, meaning "the gift of all."

When Zeus presented her, wonder took hold of the gods and men when they beheld her. It is said from her, the first woman, comes the race of women who are an evil to men, and said to have a nature to do evil.

Yet was it really an evil nature or only her curiosity that was the source of all misfortune?

It is said that the gods presented Pandora with a box into which each had put something harmful. They forbade her ever to open it.

Then they sent her to Epimethius, who took her gladly although Prometheus had warned him never to accept anything from Zeus.

In time, Pandora had to know what was in the box.

One day she lifted the lid and out flew plagues innumerable – sorrow and mischief for mankind. In terror, Pandora clapped the lid down, but it was too late.

The story parallels the creation story in the *Bible*. After the creation of the world, a helpmate is created out of man, for man. This wo-man becomes a suitable partner for the man, thus they become as one. The man and woman live in the Garden of Eden with only one restriction. The tree of the Knowledge of Good and Evil is the "Pandora's box" in *Genesis*. The correlations are outstanding when the passages are interpreted in the Universal Language of Mind, the language with which the inner mind communicates.

Both Pandora and Genesis' woman (who upon leaving the Garden will be known as Eve) represent the conscious, waking mind of every spirit, whether in a male or female body. This is far beyond the limitations of seeing the passage as fodder for feminists and chauvinists. The Universal Language of Mind affords a spiritual interpretation of very spiritual scriptures. Truth that is universal elevates awareness, rising above temporary holes in mankind's understanding. No matter what form of body may look back at you in the mirror, the woman in these symbolic stories is *you*.

Pandora and Eve both represent the outer mind that has the power to create. By opening the box, or eating from the tree, each become aware of something previously unknown. We have exercised a power for which we are now responsible. That power is reasoning. Like a child left unattended we do because we can and now we must learn to do because we think, we understand, we envision.

The first inexperienced attempts wield imagined limitations, the plagues Pandora unleashes. It will remain true for Reasoning Man for thousands of years, imagined limitations are what cause the misfortunes and the ills that we experience individually and collectively.

We, at this stage of evolution, do have a safety guard, a way to insure that we can grow and can gain understanding from misfortune. Symbolically it is the fiery, revolving sword at the gate of the Garden. The sword is a Law known as Karma. It is not a man-made law, it is the expression of the Law of Cause and Effect which permeates our universe. Everything in our universe is subject to

Cause and Effect. Every soul who has taken on physical form, chosen the physical world as their place of learning and progression, is subject to Karma.

Karma is a Sanskrit word meaning "action". The concept of Karma is an indebtedness to Self. Your Karma is what you owe your soul for the privilege of experiencing physical life. This debt is most easily described as the understandings that make up a creator.

Neither good nor bad, karma is the means by which the soul is assured of progression. Your inner self, your subconscious mind or soul can be likened to a puzzle, with pieces to be fitted together. At the present stage in our evolution we are unlocking reasoning and preparing for intuitive, Spiritual Man. Many of the pieces are already put into place. For those considering reincarnation as a truth, the pieces have been placed through hundreds perhaps thousands of lifetimes. We come back into the physical experience with a new conscious mind in order to fit in those pieces that have yet to be placed. As we do so, as Eve's serpent revealed to her, *"God knows well the moment you eat of it, your eyes will be opened and you will be like god."* And so we have had the means to become like God, to be compatible to our spiritual parent, ever since we began thinking on our own, developing conscious reasoning. The revealing of talent, of genius, of mystical experience, of Enlightenment is the natural evolution of all humanity. It is the product of God-like understandings in the hands of a spirit reaching for the wisdom of maturity.

There is a more to the story of Pandora. When she opened up the box and all these terrible whirlwind things flew out, there was one thing left in box.

The one thing left in the box was hope.

The word hope is from the Latin word *cupio* which means "to desire". Think about hope. The word is described as a desire of some good, and even more than that it's accompanied by an expectation of that good.

Hope is a confidence in the future.

Hope is trust.

All the great masters and teachers throughout the history of the world have brought hope to mankind. They did this because they lived their lives according to the great Law of Creation. This principle of creation is the foundation upon which our universe lives and moves and has its being. In the *Bible* that law is stated as, *"Seek ye first the kingdom of Heaven and all else will be given unto you."*

The lives of Spiritual Masters were a living example of the Law of Abundance. They believed that as they aided others to prosperity and abundance, they would also experience prosperity and abundance. Any teacher can tell you the Truth of this Law. As you teach, you realize just how much you know. Not only were the Masters' lives a manifestation of that law, but they taught their disciples and their followers the same. That's why we can remember them because in almost all cases it is not the Master who wrote their teachings, but rather the disciples and the followers of those teachings.

Confucius, one of these great master teachers, brought a hope to the world. The hope Confucius brought to the world is to venerate the past into a glorious future. To know more about him you'll want to research *The Analects*, an exceptional Holy work based on his teachings for the superior man.

Lao Tzu, a contemporary of Confucius, brought a hope also. His hope is in the continuity of existence beyond our physical life. Eternal life. Much of his teachings appear in the *Tao Te Ching*.

Zarathustra, the Persian Christ, brought a hope. That hope is of discrimination, to be able to separate and identify good and evil so the power of reasoning can be unleashed. If you want to know more about Zarathustra, read the *Zend-Avesta.*

Guatama, who became the Buddha, brought a hope. His hope is relinquishing desires in order to be enlightened. To know more, you'll want to read the *Dhammapada* and investigate his Eightfold Path.

Jesus of Nazareth became the Christ. His hope is to become whole and perfect as our Heavenly Father. His teachings and miraculous healings that restored others to wholeness are recorded in the *New Testament* of the *Bible.*

Hope is what each Great Master offers the waiting humanity of any time, and any place that they appear. Hope is what leads us to imagine what we can be. It is the power to believe in the inherent goodness in us all.

As the forces of the universe move, Earth is moving away from the influences of the constellation of Pisces and toward those of Aquarius. The astronomical and the astrological change, affects the planet as assuredly as our moon pull the tides of Earth's oceans. Increasing numbers of people are manifesting awareness of this change, individually and collectively. This influence is not just individual, it affects everybody, and the entire creation.

The change is most evident in the way humanity is seeking spiritual leadership and guidance in ways that are new and different from earlier times. The School of Metaphysics exists to provide spiritual leadership and guidance for all of mankind, not just a select few, but for anyone. We teach spiritual teachers.

At a teachers conference some time ago, I noted something that occurs in many places and contexts. It can occur at the workplace, in the home, or at school. As people were introducing themselves, they were asked to respond to whether or not they had completed an assignment. As I saw and listened to the responses, I was impressed in a variety of ways. Sometimes I experienced a joy and a type of recognition of learning, and at other times I experienced a disheartening dejection.

When someone would say "I fulfilled the assignment," "I accomplished it," there was a real sharing of joy because that person had moved forward. I was able to share with them in that. My life and the lives of others, were enriched because they had become prosperous.

For those who stood up and said I did not fulfill the assignment there was a sadness I experienced because I know that our everyday physical life is a place where we practice fulfilling the assignments of our souls. Failing in outer tasks usually means we are equally failing inwardly. The assignment of the soul is not something given by a teacher. It is not something given by a boss or by someone who supervises you. This assignment is akin to the individual's Karma, almost a partner.

The soul who you are came to Earth for specific purposes. Some were based upon what is lacking in your inner understanding, the hope that this life will bring resolution, a paying of the karmic debt to self. Other purposes were based upon the understandings you already possess within the fibre of your being. Your soul intended to put these understandings to use for the greater good of yourself and others. To respond is to do your dharma in life. Dharma is the assignment for a lifetime given by your soul. It is your duty that is to be fulfilled. How you approach work in your outward life reveals whether you are acting in alignment with the desires of your soul.

Your duty is to use all of those puzzle pieces you already have, all of those understandings that you as an individual have worked so long and so hard to gain. To draw upon "inherent" talents and wisdom. Maybe you're not aware of what those are yet. Maybe you are just beginning to awaken them. Apart from your awareness and application of them, they are your wealth. Those understandings are what make you unique. They bring to you and everyone you meet a richness.

Those individuals who have awareness and a commitment to fulfilling their soul's assignment readily adapt to Spiritual Renaissance. They stand out in a crowd. They think differently than the average. They are progressive in their thoughts, ideas, and practices. They live their ideals, and their ideals are evolved, reflecting Truths that touch all our lives.

The School of Metaphysics is comprised of these types of people, from all walks of life, all backgrounds, all religions and intellectual disciplines. People who believe in pursuing Enlightenment through personal excellence and spiritual disciplines. This School has an assignment. One that cannot be accomplished by a single person. Until now this assignment has been accomplished by individual, Great Masters throughout time and in different places on Earth. At humanity's present stage of evolution – moving from Reasoning, Animal Man into Intuitive, Spiritual Man – it is time for this assignment to be assumed by many.

This is the visionary mission of the School of Metaphysics.

There are many who are prepared inwardly to accept the assignment. The assignment is to unlock the power of reasoning so that intuition can become fully functional. It is to bring out the Christ principle, the Buddha principle, the Cosmic consciousness, in any individual because it exists right now in you and in me. We need only mature our consciousness to realize it.

One who is self aware is willing to move past limitations. He or she is willing to admit misfortune and put it in its proper perspective so that hope can be perceived. There may have been times that you were in situations where you were bereft with hopelessness. You would look and there was no hope to be found.

Maybe quitting was the only answer that you could see. Quitting your job. Ending your marriage. Escaping your trouble through drugs or denial. The problem is even when you quit the hopelessness remained because you misinterpreted what was before you. You began to drown in Pandora's troubles, blaming, pitying, denying.

There are times in life when you just don't see a light at the end of the tunnel. As a comfort during those times, let us meditate for illumination. Let us not be distracted by our lacks, rather, let us contemplate hope. Let us learn what brings hope into existence.

In pondering and meditating upon this query, the best insight I have received is a power each of us possesses. It is a power we've had since we were brought into existence as spirit. It is a power that manifests itself through every level of consciousness. It is a power that at any time, at any moment, you can draw upon.

This power is the power of love.

Every night at 10:30 p.m. Central Time a Circle of Love is created. It may be formed by students in a School of Metaphysics in the heartland of the United States. It may be formed by school children in India, or a group of health practitioners in England, or a family in Texas.

A Circle of Love is a practice that illuminates the individual, the world, and the universe with love. Every time a Circle of Love is created, every time it is joined with other circles spreading across the globe, hope is brought to every part of creation.

Whenever we expand light and love throughout the universe, we cause a change in the vibration of God.

A change we call Spiritual Renaissance.

There are many possible explanations: fate, destiny, chance, coincidence, providence.... To live in a better world in the next millennium will require introspection that produces understanding and wisdom that guides actions. We must think more deeply about what we cause to happen, and about our response to what others cause.

World Karma
& the Centennial Olympics

an essay first published in August 1996

It is early morning on Saturday, July 27th as I write this. The news of a bomb explosion at the Olympic Centennial Park in downtown Atlanta, Georgia, shocks me as well as the rest of the world. I listen to the eyewitness accounts of horror, the unflinching resolve of athletes and promoters to continue, the outrage and sadness of people from this country and others around the world.

Yes, such acts are those of cowardice. They are the result of madness, whether born of an evil egotism or a genetic flaw. They are an explosion of malignancy in the body of humanity. The perpetrator we describe as a terrorist because such a person seeks to create terror by destroying what another holds valuable. Whether a husband beating his wife or children, a vengeful, fired employee returning to hurt his boss, or a hired killer who plants a bomb for political reasons. The terrorist inflicts pain. He [or she] throws everyone affected into the same place of madness where he resides. What happens next determines whether karma is fulfilled or perpetuated.

Karma is a Sanskrit word describing the Universal Law of Cause and Effect. Karma is caused by thought, the intention behind the act, and it is relieved by understanding, the coming to terms with what you have caused another to experience. Every experience is caused by the quality of our thinking; benevolent or hostile, virtuous or wicked, rich or poor, positive or negative. Experience is individual, and most often collective. And so it is with karma. Karma is always individual, an "indebtedness to self", but when several or many people with a similar debt to pay gather together what is often called group karma results.

During the Olympic games the attention of the world is drawn to what is best about us — the contests to determine the finest athletes on the planet held in the country which symbolizes the greatest and longest-lived experiment in a democratic republic ever attempted by mankind. We expect our freedom in the United States. And maybe one of the karmic lessons for this country to learn is to respect our freedoms as much as we demand them.

Initially the media are drawing comparisons between this terrorism and the Olympic terrorism in Munich in 1972. They may be relevant but they are not the same. The 1972 killing of Israeli athletes and coaches by Palestinians was a manifestation of the group karma between two long-standing enemies. Although the rest of the world became part of the experience, most of us viewed it from a distance. The terrorism in Munich was specific. It involved the athletes. It involved political conflict in the Middle East. The 1996 terrorism is different. With billions of people watching, this a coward involving not a specialized group but rather the public at large. This bomb was not directed at the athletes, but to those who support the idea, who came wanting to be a part of the festivities in a free, public venue. The explosion was nondiscriminatory. It harmed young and old, rich and poor, Norwegian and Chinese, Indian and American. This terrorism was generic, it was intended to hurt the universal soul.

The explosion in Olympic Park affected us all, everyone in the world. Those reporting the event made sure we "felt" it through the images and sounds they chose to broadcast through the air. We felt the pain, the confusion, the sadness, the fear. And we felt the resolve, courage, determination, and empathy. Yet we must go beyond our feelings. We must understand our emotional reactions, placing them in perspective so understanding can surface. We must answer "why?"

No doubt by the time you read this, many of the external whys will be revealed as the perpetrator is identified and the motives made known. The more important whys involve each of us — those who were injured, those present but not harmed, those of us who watched at a distance thinking it could have been us. There are many possible explanations: fate, destiny, chance, coincidence, providence. Perhaps this unconscionable act against the world will cause us all to stop, think, evaluate, and understand. None of us are innocent bystanders. Nor are we victims. To live in a better world in the next millennium will require introspection that produces understanding and wisdom that guides actions. We must think more deeply about what we cause to happen, and about our response to what others cause. The individual karmic debts we all must, and will, pay in the privacy of our own hearts.

And what about the more universal karma? Within hours the story of what happened swept the globe. Is there understanding humanity as a whole can hope to glean from such a heinous experience? After deep reflection, I wonder if the karmic ties revolve around the Olympic Games themselves. The Olympics have brought the world together for a century now. Almost 200 countries sent representatives to the Atlanta games. But consider, do the Olympic Games truly reflect the best humanity can offer? We like to think so but what about "exercise-induced asthma" — just one of the new self-imposed diseases arising from trying to push the body beyond its capabilities. What about the use of steroids — chemical cheating in order to bring home a medal. What about injured athletes who still feel compelled to compete or silver medalists who feel they are failures? What about hired, professional athletes? Or the role of corporate sponsors. Has love for excellence, camaraderie, and learning been superseded by the love of money, the "root of all evil?"

Perhaps the world karma is simply the need to evaluate our intentions, individually and collectively. Perhaps it is time we care as much for the soul as we do the body, the spiritual as the material, the metaphysical as the physical. What I find ironic are the parallels between the 1996 Centennial Olympic Games and the 1993 Parliament of the World's Religions. The games were attended by hundreds of thousands and made televised for hours each day to an estimated 4 billion worldwide. The Parliament was attended by 7500 and poorly covered by the media. This implies a spiritually destitute global community whose priorities are entertainment and sport. It reflects a physically-engrossed perspective the entire world subscribes to. Is it any wonder that we approach the new millennium with far more trepidation and anxiety than hope and joy? What brings us together must be more than just physical achievement, physical prowess, physical competition. It is time to view the Olympics as a springboard, a beginning for world unity, the first not the last. The games have been a physical stimulus for sharing human drama. Now perhaps they will find transcendent purpose becoming a spiritual stimulus for our soul progression.

Mythologies across the world point to major calamities during this time of transition. Most people believe these will be natural events beyond their control; earthquakes, weather storms, tidal waves. Others believe the disasters will be in man's hands - nation against nation, political wars - but out of their own. Most people hold this same idea of helplessness about karma. Que sera, sera; what will be, will be.

Who would have thought that in a bombing during the Olympics we would see a manifestation of prophecy? How we think about this event, and the response we make, will shape our lives individually and collectively.

With a change of heart the world can cure the hatred and heal its malignancy.

With an expanded vision, the world can pay its karmic debt and look forward to the transformations ahead with clarity and kindness.

IV

The Spiritual Renaissance

Birth

"Reason respects the difference, and imagination, the similitudes of things."

– English poet Percy Bysshe Shelley (1792-1822)

"I cannot imagine myself living without religion. I could as easily fancy a living body without a heart. To one who is deaf and blind, the spiritual world offers no difficulty. Nearly everything in the natural world is as vague, as remote from my sense, as spiritual things seem to the minds of most people. But the inner or mystic sense, if you like, gives me vision of the unseen."

– Helen Keller, American memoirist & essayist, (1880-1968)

Spiritual Birth
Kundalini & the Mystical Child

This is a partial transcript of my address during the 1993 Parliament of the World's Religions on Spiritual Initiation: Gateways to Awareness

I am sure that you share with me a great joy in being here. It is such an honor and privilege for me to be able to be here and to address you today, to share some of the things I've found to be true.

I think what we are all seeking, by being at this centennial Parliament of the Worlds' Religions, is Truth. Truths that we can all live; Truths that are universal.

Part of what I teach is the Truths in all the Holy Scriptures of the world. All the great masters who came to us in the past and that come to us now, are imparting their wisdom of why we exist, not only in a body, but as a mind and as a spirit. The teachings that they offer us apply to anyone, anywhere, at any time.

One of the things that has impressed me during this Parliament is when I go to any of the Buddhist's or the Hindu talks, the commencement of the gathering is the chanting of the vibration of Om. *Om* is the vibration of creation. I use that vibration personally in my own solitude and meditations as a point of helping me to reach states of transcendental consciousness. I have realized by being a part of these presentations and talks, that when this vibration is used, it centers the energy of all and any in its vicinity. It calms the mind of all within its reach.

With this in mind, I invite you to chant the Om with me. As it resonates throughout your being I want you to remember this because we'll be recalling it in a few moments.

[We chanted Om for several minutes, which I would encourage you to do now. Sound the vibration aloud, striving to sound the *F* note on the piano scale. Allow the vibration to start in the chest and rise up through the throat floating out the mouth as the energy emanates from the heart upward and out the crown of the head.]

The critical issues that face each one of us in our personal lives as well as humanity together are the essence of discussion at this Parliament. The questions that divide us — the questions of racism, of sexism, of poverty, of conflict and hatred — are ones that we are hearing repeatedly during this Parliament. I've heard these expressed in many different ways by many different people in the last few days, as probably you have as well. What has come to my mind is a quote by Confucius. In his teachings, he said:

> *" To put the world in order, you must first put*
> *the nation in order.*
> *To put the nation in order, you must first put*
> *the family in order.*
> *To put the family in order, you must first put*
> *your personal self right.*
> *You must set your heart right."*

Throughout this Parliament I think we are witnessing a deepening awareness upon each individual's part of who we are; not only as a physical being, as a person from a particular country or of a particular race or religious creed, but a person indeed of humanity or of humankind.

In that kind of awareness, we have the seeds that will be able to cause us to be transformed and to transcend the limitations that we all tend to experience in our lives. Indeed we have the seed of transcending the current divisions brought about by reasoning and enter into a spiritual renaissance unlike any mankind has known before.

Throughout Eastern scriptures the division is referred to as a separateness, or the dualism, the pairs of opposites. The love and the hate. The war and the peace. The male and the female. There is an awareness of awakening that has been taught by all the great masters of all religions throughout history. The message from each of them is to awaken. It is as if we have a sleeping consciousness when we experience in a physical world. And our confusion and our doubts and our limitations begin to overrun us. We feel separate; we feel separate from each other, we feel separate from our God, we feel separate from ourselves, and its hard to reach through that.

Yet it has been done. It can be done.

In order to transcend that separateness, the message has been to awaken in consciousness. There's a very exciting awakening that's occurring right now. I am reminded of the *Bhagavad Gita* when it speaks about faith. It talks about each man and his faith denoting his own concept of deity. Whatever your faith is, whatever you believe in, is your concept of deity. It reflects your character. It reflects the essence of who you really are. And in being able to understand that, a man's concept of God is *"himself at his best magnified to infinity."* Likewise a man's devil is *"himself at his worst, magnified to infinity."* If we are to know the Real Self or the real man then we look to see what his deities are.

I thoroughly believe that it is time for religion and science to come together, to unite. I thoroughly believe that it is time for faith to unite with action, so that there can be a transcendence. I believe that we are on the threshold of what I call spiritual maturity. We've gone through a phase of being the infant where we relied upon spiritual teachers or masters or leaders to give us rules, to give us dogmas, to give us ways that we could live righteously. And we've entered into a time of science for the last century which has permeated our lives in many ways. This is truly a time of spiritual adolescence. We have stretched the limits, tested the boundaries of what we can physically do. We have met ourselves as a physical creator, sometimes forgetting or ignoring our spiritual origin. Yet in truth we have not left the religion, we have added on to it.

With scientific knowledge, we now have the question before us of when we terminate someone's life—not through anger or hatred but through disconnecting the life support systems we have chosen to employ to prolong that life. We have scientific clairvoyance and capacity to change the genetic code of the physical body while it's still in the womb. These are god-like issues that confront us now. The kinds of experimentations that we do scientifically, the kinds of wisdom and judgement that we bring to those choices, will determine the quality of life for each of us as individuals as well as humanity.

These issues are awakening within us a sense of responsibility as freedom, a sense of recognizing that we're reaching toward a spiritual adulthood. The awakening cannot be escaped, it is happening. It is an individual happening. I want to talk about it today in a specific way. Physically, according to the physical DNA of the physical body, around the age of thirteen, the body undergoes hormonal changes which activate chemical changes in the body, enabling the female to begin the onset of menstruation, and the male to begin to produce potent sperm. Therein for every individual there is the ability to procreate physically. There is the ability to create something from ourselves — a physical child.

In the East, they speak of *Kundalini* and this is a word that is not in the American vernacular. It derives its name from a Hindu goddess, Kundala, which means coiled. She represents creative energy. The same creative energy that is used to manifest a physical body, or a child. But in this case, this energy is used and is channeled toward enlightenment. Instead of that energy being channeled out into the physical to create and unite a sperm and an egg to create a physical body, those energies, those juices, those chemicals, physically are to be channelled up the spine and to the head. This is what creates mystical experiences. This is what creates enlightenment.

For some people this rising of the Kundalini can create states of disorientation, states of confusion. But it is the state of the genius —the artist, the writer—who creates from a kind of inspiration that seems to come from its own bidding, its own will. And yet that essence of creative frenzy or ecstasy is a mark of mystical experience that is stimulated through the Kundalini.

The enlightenment that is evidenced by all the great masters and teachers of the world is a mastery of Kundalini energy. It goes beyond the genius, beyond the talented, and into the realms of uniting separation into transforming individual consciousness into a cosmic consciousness, or a Christ consciousness, or a Buddha consciousness. It is the awareness of the extension of what is beyond you; of contributing yourself, your life, your energy to something that is much greater than you.

These experiences, these mystical experiences, happen within your life every day. You may not recognize them, but I am certain in your life that there have been mystical moments. There have been moments when you have had a sense of urgency. This urgency was not about something that you needed to be about at a certain time. It was a sense of urgency *within* you that was rising that perhaps compelled you to speak to someone, or to touch someone, to go somewhere for a purpose that you didn't really know consciously until you actually arrived there. Or perhaps you've experienced times of a sense of duty, a sense of obligation, a sense of having a mission, something that was very important that you are here to accomplish.

Perhaps you've had a near death experience, where your physical life almost ended. There are so many people who can tell you of experiences, who can share experiences, where clinically they were scientifically declared dead. But their consciousness returns. And the stories time after time, no matter who the person is, no matter where they lived, no matter what their background, include seeing a light . At some point they saw a light. They may have moved through a tunnel toward a light; they may have moved through a cave. But they are reaching toward a light.

One of the most profound awarenesses that come from that mystical "near-death" experience is not only the release of the fear of dying, but more importantly, a sense that what we're here for is to love one another. Those mystical experiences touch our hearts, our mind, our souls, and transform our entire spirit. So from that day forward nothing is ever the same again. For many women the birth of a child produces this, where there's such ecstasy but such pain at the arrival of a child. At that moment the consciousness is aligned and a mystical experience is had and nothing is ever quite the same again.

In mystical experience there is a sense of an altering of time and space. And many times what derives from this is the ability for precognition. Sometimes it comes in what people would probably describe as visions or inclinations; sometimes it is revealed in nighttime dreams. But precognition is one of the advantages, one of the rewards, of spiritual transcendence, or mystical experience.

All of these I see as steps along the road. I see them as leading us to what I see as the destiny of each of us, of all of mankind, and that is enlightenment. It is the state of illumination, where we are aware of our individuality. We are also aware of everything, of the all. There is autonomy without separation. Diversity with unity. Those types of mystical experiences are the "something" to seek in your own life and in the lives of people around you.

The channeling of the Kundalini energy, that creative energy, up the spine and to the brain, creates a flow of chemical juices. In the *Vedas* it is referred to as soma, in the *Bible* it is referred to as

Euphrates, for the alchemist it was the rosa. What Kundalini creates is the birth of a mystical child. I spoke of channeling the Kundalini down the spine and out into the physical to create a physical body for a newly incarned child but when the Kundalini is channeled upward it creates the mystical child.

It's the Greek story of Persephone and the serpent.

It's the Biblical story of Mary and the virgin birth.

It's the birth of Horace by Isis. Horace was conceived by God.

The birth of the mystical child is in all the spiritual literature throughout the world. Researching such literature is such an exciting investigation when you are looking for truth. It is important to hear what others have to say about such writings. It is important to listen to one other. It is important that we give and receive.

Yet the kind of awareness that you can receive by actually reading the writings — no matter if they are four hundred centuries old or if they are four thousand centuries old — is unsurpassed for you begin to see the unity of the truth that is universal and it begins to absorb within you......

.....Mystical experiences are produced by a combination of mental, physical, and spiritual factors. Jesus, Gautama, Zarathustra, Lao Tzu, Mohammed, all the great spiritual teachers of the world experienced pure consciousness and enlightenment. There are two products of an active Kundalini energy. One is those who have achieved enlightenment. And the other are those who display genius. If you'll think about it, it is to these two groups of people that we can attribute all of the advancements of mankind.

The energy of Kundalini, the creative energy that man possesses, can be understood and it can be harnessed. It cannot be induced; it cannot be forced. Some people try to force it through the use of drugs or chemically changing the physical body so that the brain is affected thus producing hallucinations or visions or an altering of the consciousness. As soon as the drug wears off, the body seeks to restore its natural chemistry. Many times these chemicals cause disconnections in the nervous system of the brain with lingering and sometimes permanent effects. Drugs are not a good way to induce mystical experience.

Some people use hypnosis. Although it can be very effective for therapy, trying to produce a mystical experience with hypnosis is to the mind what a drug is to the body. Hypnosis at best depends upon some type of intervention for what needs to be a direct experience, and at worst is artificially-influenced pretense. It is not really an effective way to produce mystical experiences that become a part of the entire being.

Some people use mantras, and although mantras are very good for focusing the mind and causing the whole Self to vibrate at a certain level, they do not provide a time of stillness in the mind so that a complete experience can be received and experienced. This is a step in the right direction, but it is not the destination. Guided meditation is very similar to the mantra experience because, although it can influence you to have a certain kind of awareness and a certain attunement with the Self, the true mystical experiences are the ones that are achieved when alone, totally in solitude. Jesus told his disciples *"to go into their closets and pray."* He didn't say to pray out in the street or in groups. He said go into your closet; go into solitude.

The kind of familiarity that occurs within the Self, the kind of peace that enables you to move through life so you can do your duty, you can do your work, is very important to attain and it can be developed. I have found through research and application there are two significant factors that are necessary for mystical experience. One of them is reasoning. Reasoning is the experience of the fundamental nature of things. It is a sequence of events of the movement of thought. Therefore it can be learned. And it can be taught. The second is intuition. Intuition is the direct grasp of truth; being able to incorporate into your being the fundamental structure of the universe. Intuition is also a sequence of events. It can also be learned. And it can also be taught. This type of learning and teaching is what I have devoted my adult life to, and it is the mission of the School of Metaphysics.

I think as we become aware of these universal principles and we dedicate ourselves to spiritual practice we will find mystical experiences occurring more often in our lives and they will be much more useful. The head of the Catholic Church, Pope John Paul II visited our country this past summer during World Youth Day. I followed the parts of his visit covered by the media. I was very impressed by several accounts I read. I brought some with me that I'd like to share with you in case you haven't heard. Reporters interviewed some of the youngsters there, those embarking on their teenage years whose Kundalini energy has now become very active. One of them said that she was thoroughly impressed by the "total love in the air." This among a group of people over ten times the size of this Parliamentary gathering. Another said, "I'm not used to people being nice to me. The real world is a bit tough." This remains with me. It spoke to me about how *you* and *I* see ourselves and each other and what *we* teach our children. It said something about how *we* tend to live. What it said was a world where enlightenment, and love, and dignity, and integrity, and cooperation, and union, and all of the things we value in life, that we hold to be important, is not a real world....

But it is. All the strife that we've experienced, the differences we've experienced, don't last. They're temporal in nature, because they are not part of our spirit. I truly believe that as we learn to be responsive to this energy that we have available to us, as we conceive our adulthood spiritually, we'll find our greatest hope is how we teach ourselves, how we raise ourselves and our children—in awareness.

The newly incarned soul, comes to you, a physical parent, for guidance and instruction on how to live a physical life. The child seeks knowledge of what needs to be done for physical survival. But there is also parental responsibility to the soul of that individual who comes to you for *spiritual* guidance and instruction. I think that as we respond to this in ourselves as well as each other, and with other children, we'll find the hope of humanity is the harnessing of our own creative energies and the unfoldment of our own spiritual maturity.

Words have meaning. They reflect what is created in the mind. As a child I learned the rhyme "sticks and stones may break my bones but words will never hurt me". It is a good rule to live by because it teaches proper perspective.

Reaping What We Sow

Media, particularly electronic media of television which comes into our homes, is our era's storyteller. In every society ever known on earth there have been those who learn and recite histories, both real and imagined, to the group. In every society they are welcomed, even revered. They are the reporters of what is occurring, the interpreters of the meaning of our existence, and sometimes the purveyors of eternal truth.

As in all societies there are good storytellers and there are bad storytellers. Those worth lending your ear to, those not worth your time. Those who uplift even when chastising, those who spread discord with their verbal poison. Sometimes it is difficult to tell the difference between these two, but eventually the truth is always revealed.

This is happening to television. Rather than uniting us, it is progressively dividing us. With the advent of satellite television, whatever your interests there is a signal beaming from the heavens just for you. Science fiction. Twenty four hour news. Romance. Nostalgia. Westerns. Avant Garde films. Whether seeking information, stimulation, or diversion you can find it on tv. You can also find the good storytellers and the bad.

I came across an example of the latter in those quick vignettes of sensory overload we call commercials. A beautiful child filmed in cheesecloth appeared on the screen accompanied by soothing music. Her young equally attractive mother picked her up, cradling the child in her arms, while an intrusive male voice intoned, "Look at her. Could you lie to her?" I was shocked. Yes, it got my attention, and I eagerly expected a refreshing and instructive moral that would uplift the standards of anyone listening. I expected good story telling. What I got was the bad.

Somewhere in the eighties "I lied" became fashionable in our society. Seems like it sprouted from "The Terminator" or some other movie of its calibre. Immediately there were imitators, mostly teens and men who thought it clever. But within a few short years it spread until now we are being encouraged to lie to our own infants. Lighten up, you say? The first time you hear a pun it is funny, upon repeated hearing it loses its charm. And charm is perhaps what it is all about. We can be too easily charmed by what seems attractive but causes it harm.

"I lied" was at first funny. It was vogue. It was chic, reflecting a cocky self-assurance that you got away with something, pulled one over on someone else. You won. A societal habit of cuteness garnered at the expense of someone else.

Words have meaning. They reflect what is created in the mind. As a child I learned the rhyme "sticks and stones may break my bones but words will never hurt me". It is a good rule to live by because it teaches proper perspective. It says when someone wishes you ill you need not accept it. You never have to absorb someone else's bad attitudes. Others can only hurt you when you allow them to, when you give them the power. "Fear not the man who can kill the body, fear the one who can kill the soul." That's what our acceptance of "I lied" is doing, killing the soul of humanity.

We must restore perspective. Evolving, learning, fortifying, changing self.

We must make our ideas and our words match. This has been a personal ideal for me for two decades, ever since I learned the aligning of the two is the key to communication. Failing in this is reason why children do not respect their parents, and adults in general. "Do as I say not as I do" is the cry of an adolescent not an adult. An adolescent, whether they have lived 13 years or 50, should not produce a child they are not prepared to parent.

When thoughts and words match, there is no need for government to function as a pseudo-parent. Because the two have been at odds in the U.S. since the Great Depression, our government has become the societal equivalent of the adolescent. Our governing is determined by peer pressure. Laws reflect general opinions - "conventional wisdom," journalists call it. An obvious example of this government by popular opinion is slow descent of acceptance toward smoking tobacco. In the 1930's and 1940's cigarettes were everywhere. The epitome of romance was a male lighting a female's cigarette. By the '50's it was a bad habit indulged in by hoods and beatniks. By the '60's it was socially acceptable. In the '70's, the Surgeon General warned cigarettes *might be* health hazards and ads were banned on - television! The '80's the forces against it were uniting, by the '90's smoking bans in first government offices and then privately owned businesses spread across the country.

The irony is while tobacco fell out of favor, the drumbeat of approval to legalize marijuana, a substance at least equally toxic to the body and the mind, was growing.

An even greater irony is how the overblown tobacco debate is an "I lied" idea. After all, smoking is much less a health hazard than the overall chemical dependency in this country. If you are offended, look in your medicine chest and you'll come face to face with why.

The great lie is the refusal to clean up our own act while trying to force someone else to clean up theirs. It's as if we convince ourselves we are doing some great good by being hypocrites. We are not. The first house to put in order is your own. "Take the plank out of your own eye before you endeavor to take the twig from your brother's."

It is clear that as a society we have yet to learn to bring our thoughts and actions into alignment.

But this is a lesson we will learn. In the near future.

The concept of fashionable lying did not begin with a movie, although because of its wide spread appeal and viewing, the movie did stimulate large numbers of us to mimic what we saw. If we missed the movie, we imitated friends who mimicked the movie.

"I lied" occurred in the '60's. I remember as a high school student, all of a sudden we were served something other than fish for Friday lunch. I like fish so I wondered why.

I learned the reason we had fish every Friday was for the Catholics. An idea that no doubt someone nowadays would file some civil rights law suit over, impaling themselves on the twig in their own eye.

I remember asking a few of my Catholic friends why they were supposed to eat fish on Friday. They didn't know. It was just against their religion. It was a practice they'd grown up with but the spirit of the law had been long lost. Most times their parents didn't know the reason so they couldn't teach it. As an adult studying religion, I would learn the concept beyond the letter of the law they practiced like modern-day Pharisees.

What was troubling to me was all of a sudden one day it stopped.

As if all of a sudden the concept had no meaning anymore. It was like God had changed his mind.

When public opinion dictates truth we're in trouble. Be it in government, but especially in religious matters.

Truth is too rare a commodity. Too valuable to treat carelessly.

When I was a child I believed no matter where I'd hide, God would see me, he would be there. And so I gave up the temptation to lie. Even as my idea of an omnipresent God evolved, I learned lying has its own consequences, always.

Getting caught is not the chief worry for liars. When and how is. What you put out does return to you, often manyfold. As you sow, so do you reap. It is the lesson of the adolescent at any age.

V

The Spiritual Renaissance

Awakening

"Often when looking at a mass of things for sale,
he would say to himself,
'How many things I have no need of.' "

– Socrates, Greek philosopher (469-399 BC)

"You give but little when you give of your possessions.
It is when you give yourself that you truly give."

–Kahlil Gibran, Syrian-American mystic & poet (1883-1931)

Spiritual Awakening
A Life Worth Living

Based upon an Interfaith sermon first given in August, 1994.

Once there was a fisherman who lived with his wife in a small cottage near a river. Every day the fisherman went to the river and cast his net into the water to harvest dinner.

One day the fisherman caught a magical fish in his net. He knew the fish was magical because when it spoke to him. "Fisherman, I beg you to let me live. I am not really a fish, I am an enchanted prince. Please let me swim away."

Say no more," said the fisherman. "I am quite willing to set free a fish that can talk!"

"For that, I will grant you a wish," said the fish. The fisherman said there was nothing he needed.

The fisherman let the fish go free. When he went home, his wife asked, "Husband, what have you caught for me to cook for our dinner?"

"I haven't brought anything home," he said. "I caught a big fish who said he was an enchanted prince, so I threw him back into the water."

"My!" she said. "You might at least have made a wish before you set him free!"

"What would I wish for?" asked her husband.

"Well, we certainly could use a nicer place to live. I'm sure that if you go back and ask the fish for a nicer house, he will gladly give it to you!"

The fisherman did not really think that they needed a nicer house, but he loved his wife and so the next day he went to the river and called:

"Princely fish that I set free,
Hear my words and come to me."

The fish soon appeared. The fisherman said, "My wife would like to make a wish if you would be so kind to grant it."

"What is this wish?" asked the fish.

"She is tired of living in a little cottage," said the fisherman. "She would like to live in nicer home."

"Go home to your wife," said the fish. "She already has her wish."

The fisherman hurried back home.

There was his wife waving from the doorway of a nice new house. The house was filled with everything the fisherman and his wife could possibly need. "Now we can be happy," the fisherman said.

But a few days later the wife said, "Husband, this house is too small. We need more space for all these lovely things! Go back to the river and ask the fish for a castle!"

The fisherman wanted his wife to be happy so he returned to the river and called:

"Princely fish that I set free,
Hear my words and come to me."

"Now what?" asked the fish.

"Alas, my wife wants to live in a castle," said the fisherman regretfully.

"Go home. She is already there," said the fish.

When the fisherman returned home, his wife waved to him from the balcony of a huge castle. Its rooms were full of golden furniture, and the tables were filled with wonderful things to eat.

"Isn't everything beautiful?" asked the wife. The fisherman agreed. He was sure that now they had everything they could ever possibly need.

But early the next morning, the wife woke up frowning.

She said, "Husband, we live in a castle, so we should be king and queen of all the land."

The fisherman didn't want that at all, but his wife insisted. The unhappy fisherman finally gave in and went back to the river.

Once again the fisherman called:

"Princely fish that I set free,

Hear my words and come to me."

"What is it now?" asked the fish.

"I'm afraid my wife wants us to be king and queen," sighed the fisherman.

"Go home. She is already queen," Said the fish.

Sure enough, when the fisherman arrived back at the castle, his wife was sitting on a high gold throne. "Now that you are queen," said the fisherman, "surely you will not want to wish for anything more."

"I'm not so sure of that," said the queen. "I have a feeling there is something else we need."

That night the fisherman slept well, but his wife lay awake tossing and turning and wondering about what her next wish would be.

Just as the wife was about to fall asleep the sun came up. Bright sunlight streamed in through the royal bedroom window. The wife sat up in bed.

"Husband!" she said. "I do not think the sun should be allowed to rise without my permission! Go tell the fish I want to have power over the rising and setting of the sun!"

"Wife," said the fisherman, "I think that is too much to ask!"

At this, the wife flew into a rage. "Go tell the fish to grant my wish!" she shouted.

Quaking with fear, the fisherman got dressed. He hurried out of the castle and headed toward the river. As he walked, strong winds began to blow and the river began to rage.

The fisherman stumbled to the river bank. He could barely hear his own voice over the fierce wind as he called:

"Princely fish that I set free,
Hear my words and come to me."

"What does you wife want now?" asked the fish as he rose up through the choppy waves.

"Oh, fish," said the fisherman fearfully, "she wants the power to make the sun rise and set."

"Go home to your wife," said the fish.

Suddenly, the wind stopped as quickly as it had started. The fisherman went home to find his wife in front of their humble cottage again.

"Husband," said the wife, "I am so sorry that I got carried away with greed. Each new and better thing just made me want more. But the more I got, the more unhappy I became."

"It's my fault too," the fisherman said. "When you wanted more, I asked the fish for it."

The fisherman kissed his wife, took his net, and went to the river. He gazed into the clear blue water as he fished.

That night he brought his wife a nice, plain fish for their dinner.

What determines the quality of life?

Many people think the same way the fisherman's wife does. They crave money. They crave possessions. They crave fame. They crave positions, all the while thinking that these things will bring them a sense of fulfillment. They believe in some way, these things will enhance the quality of their lives.

Such people are bound by their physical needs only, by their bodies and their senses. Their awareness is very small. They live and they die, and another incarnation comes and goes with very little soul growth accomplished.

Gautama the Buddha said this:

> *"There is no social order, no righteous leadership or kingship unless men lose themselves in something greater than themselves.*
>
> *Desire to gratify the senses, sensuousness, desire for personal immortality, desire for prosperity, worldliness, all these must be to overcome. A man must no longer be living for himself."*

There is a point in each person's individual evolution where he or she lets go of the physical desires and begins to reach for more. He or she is like the fisherman. The fisherman was no longer living for himself. This showed in his willingness to respond and try to fulfill the desires of his wife.

Many people are like the fisherman. They define the quality of their life through family or through education or through work or through government or through religion. They tend toward more awareness than the less aware person because they embrace these experiences for what they might be able to give and to receive.

They enter into a family to have sense of belonging, to experience love, to experience cooperation. They look at education as a way of learning, of adding to themselves; not merely in a physical way, but in terms of an increase in mentality.

They look at their work as a place to be creative, a place to give something of value and to receive in like kind.

They look at government as a sense of order, a sense of justice, and perhaps even a place for volunteerism, to volunteer their time to aid someone else in their life.

They look at religion as a place to have a sense of higher purpose to know that their life amounts to something beyond the point of physical birth and physical death. Such people are brought into awareness sporadically both in pleasant ways and unpleasant ways. They're continually adding some kind of new awareness to themselves, but it is erratic at best. It comes and it goes.

When we have reached the point of evolution where we have these spontaneous awarenesses of what physical life is all about, we become more mindful of the experiences in our physical life. We realize experience is more than what arrives and what leaves. Experience has a much greater purpose.

We eventually come to a point where we find that what determines the quality of life is not really as important as the qualities that make a good life. A life worth living. It's not what we do during our lives but how we do it that makes our lives what they are.

It's not the money that we can make, but it's the exchange of value, the giving and receiving that is done with money that makes a difference to the soul.

It's the usefulness of possessions that we own that makes the quality of our life, not the amassing and the hoarding of them.

It's the importance of the quality of our own way of thinking and the ideas that we entertain, not the fame or the notoriety that we may bring to ourselves. It's the influence that we have upon the lives of others to help them to abundance, to help them toward enlightenment that matters. It's not the position we hold.

It's the cooperation or the loyalty that we can experience in familial relationships, not the fact that we have a mother or a father or a son or a daughter, or a brother or a sister, or a husband or a wife.

It's the learning, the adding to ourselves, the increasing of knowledge, the potential of expansion of consciousness that is important, not the educational degrees or the institutes where we've studied.

It's the productivity of what we as individuals can bring to make life better for other people that makes the difference to the soul, not the work that we do.

It is the service we can offer to others not the action itself of volunteering or being a part of something much bigger than ourselves, but it's the action of service that makes a difference in the quality of our lives.

It's the spiritual awareness that we can embrace, that we can obtain so that we can transcend the everyday drudgery of physical life, that religion brings us.

These make life worth living.

The value, the usefulness, the importance, the influence, the cooperation, the learning, the productivity, the service, the spiritual awareness. These are the things that make life worth living because these are the qualities of a creation.

From birth Siddhartha Gautama lived in luxury in his father's palace. Every desire was fulfilled. At the age of 29, the unfulfilled desire to know what lay beyond the palace walls and gardens led him to journey the countryside. There he encountered for the first time old age, sickness, and death. The questions these new experiences brought forth within his consciousness set Gautama upon the quest of his lifetime, a quest that would culminate in his destiny.

In time, Gautama learned that the secret to life was desirelessness. His teachings include a way we can live in harmony with Universal Truth, free from misery-making attachment. His *Eightfold Path* is as relevant to each of us, even those of us in Western, material society, today as twenty-five hundred years ago. His steps are these: *Right Views, Right Aspirations, Right Speech, Right Action, Right Livelihood, Right Effort, Right Mindfulness, Right Meditation.* The steps are not linear, they are interconnected. Each emphasizes a construction of thinking essential to the whole consciousness.

The Eightfold Path is one of undivided attention; the "narrow path that will set you free" Jesus spoke of in the *Bible*. Being attentive, being present in your life, enables you to embrace each moment and give completely. These eight Buddhic concepts are so very rich, each can serve as the focal point for a hundred meditations. Each seek to direct the aspirant's thinking to the highest good. Where the highest good exists in consciousness, there is light.

Every time we court a greater awareness while in the midst of the physical activity of our lives, we cause ourselves to be that much closer to our Maker. That much closer to our God. We feel that kinship and it shines throughout every thought that we have and every action that we take. It influences. It touches the people that we greet. It makes a difference in the way we see ourselves, and the way we see life.

What's the most direct way to live a life that's worth living?

It's an important question because I know that there have been times when you have awakened in the morning and you've wondered "What am I going to do?" or you've thought, "Boy, it would be better to just roll over and go back to sleep." In other words there was nothing really important in your life that you were waking to. I know that there are needs you have, things that you think you don't have but lust for. Many people want physical things in their lives, but there is still an emptiness they experience in their own soul, in their own awareness of who they are.

What is the most direct way to live a life that's worth living?

How can we enhance the quality of life?

The way to know the Source of the qualities is to strive to know God. Many have discovered the secret of this before you and I. In the Judeo-Christian religion there are three such men who discovered it and left records of how to live, how to think so that your life can be worth living.

The first one is a man named Moses.

Moses was an exceptional person. He had constant communion with God, receiving the ten commandments, ten precepts that guarantee a life worth living.

These are Moses' words,

> *"Hear, oh Israel, the Lord our God is one Lord. Thou shalt love the Lord thy God with all thine heart, and with all thy soul, and with all thy might.*
>
> *"These words which I command thee this day shall be in thine heart and thou shalt teach them diligently unto thy children. And shalt talk of them when thou sittest in thine house and when thou walkest by the way, and when thou liest down and when thou riseth up."*

When you strive for the highest quality of life, when you wake up in the morning and come back to conscious, physical awareness, you will have a real sense that your life means something. You will know what you are to do that day. You will know that you are working and living in the service of something much greater than you.

If these things are to come to pass in your life, then you must be willing to populate your thoughts with God, with heavenly matters, with your Maker.

Moses' counsel is not to think once in a while about God. Or to think for an hour every Sunday, or for an hour every evening in meditation. Or when you want something because you don't have it. There are many people who pray for things because they don't have them. He does not counsel to think of God when there's something adverse in your life and you want to strike a bargain, "Oh please, straighten this out for me and I'll be better I promise." Those kinds of ways of thinking do not lead to a quality of life. They do not help you see that your life is worth living. Populating your thinking with God consciousness does. This is what Moses encourages.

Insuring that your consciousness awakens in Godly counsel unifies your consciousness to the common good.

There is another man who knew about the common good. His name was Solomon.

You may know him because he's reportedly the richest man in the Bible; he had absolutely everything. If you don't know his story then you probably wondered how he received such good fortune.

Solomon loved the Lord. He inherited his father David's kingdom. David's life was filled with challenge and trouble and disappointment, yet increasingly through his life he learned from his mistakes. This was Solomon's true inheritance.

Solomon sacrificed and burned incense in high places. A thousand burnt offerings did Solomon offer upon the altar at Gideon until one night the Lord appeared to Solomon in a dream saying,

> *"Ask what I shall give thee."*
>
> *Solomon said, "Thou has showed unto thy servant David, my father, great mercy." Courting as he walked before thee in truth and in righteousness and in uprightness of heart with thee. And thou has kept for him this great kindness that thou hast given him a son to sit on his throne as it is the stay.*
>
> *"And now, oh Lord my God, thou hast made thy servant king instead of David my father. I am but a little child, I know not how to go out or come in and thy servant is in the midst of thy people which thou hast chosen, a great people, that cannot be numbered nor counted for multitude.*
>
> *"Give therefore thy servant an understanding heart*

to judge thy people that I may discern between good and bad. For who is able to judge this so great a people?"

And the speech pleased the Lord that Solomon had asked this thing. And God said unto him, "Because thou hast asked this thing and hast not asked for thyself long life, neither hast asked riches for thyself, nor hast asked the life of thine enemies, but hast asked for thyself understanding to discern judgment.

"Behold, I have according to thy words, lo I have given thee a wise and understanding heart so that there was none like thee before thee, neither after thee shall any arise like unto thee. And I have also given thee that which thou hast not asked both riches and honor so that there shall not be any among the kings like unto thee all thy days.

"And if thou will walk in my ways to keep my statutes and my commandments as thy father David did walk, then I will lengthen thy days."

When God told Solomon that he could have anything he desired, Solomon said the only thing he wanted was wisdom to rule God's people. When wisdom rules your thinking, when it is all that you long for, your consciousness is expanded and you learn the secret of Solomon. You discover why he was the richest man in the *Bible*.

There was another great teacher who discovered the same secret. He talked about it in this way

"Lay not up for your souls, treasures upon earth where moth and rust doth corrupt. Where thieves break through and steal. But lay up for your souls treasures in heaven where neither moth nor rust doth corrupt and where thieves do not break through or steal. For where

your treasure is there will your heart be also.

"The light of the body is the eye, if therefore thine eye be single thy whole body shall be full of light, but if thine eye be evil, thy whole body shall be full of darkness. If therefore the light that is, is darkness, how great is that darkness.

"No man can serve two masters for either he will hate the one and love the other, or else he will hold to the one and despise the other. You cannot serve God and mammon.

"For this reason, I say to you, Do not worry for your life, what you will eat and what you will drink, nor for your body, what you will wear. Behold, is not life much more important than food, and the body than clothing?

"Observe the birds of the sky, for they do not sow, neither do they harvest nor gather in to barns, and yet your Father in heaven feeds them. Are you not much more important than they?

"Who is among you who by worrying can add one cubit to his stature?

"Why do you worry about clothing? Observe the wild flowers, how they grow; they do not get tired out, nor do they spin.

"But I say to you that not even Solomon with all of his glory was arrayed like one of them.

"Now if God clothes in such fashion the grass of the field, which today is and tomorrow falls into the fire-place, is he not much more mindful of you, O you of little faith?

"Therefore do not worry or say, What will we eat, or what will we drink, or with what will we be clothed?

"For worldly people seek after all these things. Your

Father in heaven knows that all of these things are also necessary for you.

"But seek first the kingdom of God and his righteousness and all these things shall be added to you."

Jesus devoted his life to learning to be the Christ.

Several have studied and written about his life from the time of seven to thirty, the years missing from the New Testament of the *Bible*. Most of those accounts reveal startling information concerning his willingness to travel, to learn, to study ancient wisdom in the East. There is no doubt that Jesus was an Essene, one of three major Jewish sects of the time and the one invested in studying and applying the inner truth of scriptures. The Essenes were dedicated to fulfilling prophecy, to bringing about the conditions that would bring forth the Messiah, the savior, the Christ.

Beyond these accounts, worthy of your time in pursuit, is the wonderful way these, and indeed all, holy scriptures are penned. They are much more than words. They are images, living visualizations, that when interpreted symbolically come to life. They reveal the story of everyone, every male or female who has ever lived. They reveal where we have come from, why we are here, and where we are to go.

Jesus and what he became, becomes each of us. Gautama and what he became, becomes each of us. We identify ourselves with what exists beyond the physical. Be that soul or spirit, it is in truth the thinker; the one who yearns for enlightenment, the one for whom belief no longer suffices. Only knowing will fulfill such a one. Only knowing will fulfill every desire elevating us to the state of desirelessness.

This consuming passion to know is characteristic of a renaissance man. The consuming passion to know the Creator propels such a one into spiritual renaissance.

Once the consciousness is awakened, rest will come only when the ideal is made known. Like an artist who must paint, a musician who must compose, a scientist who must experiment, a physician who must heal, now the divine compulsion is turned inward. What to those who have yet to awaken may seem an incredible waste of talent, even the abandoning of destiny is revealed on the other side as its greatest fulfillment. Fulfillment known by those who seek first the kingdom of God.

These ones are on their way to knowing what Jesus, and Gautama, and Zarathustra, and Lao Tzu, and Confucius, and other Spiritual masters who came before realized. Jesus becomes less and less a physical male who lived a remarkable life hundreds of years ago. He begins to be representative of you, the seeker who desires enlightenment. And in that way his life reveals what can be for each of us. From his humble birth signifying the awakening of consciousness to Christ potential to his ministry symbolizing a mature understanding of our universe to his death and resurrection, the transformation to spiritual consciousness, we become the one awakening to a powerful destiny.

Anytime we seek counsel in any holy scripture, we find something glorious and that is the way to live a very full life. Ralph Waldo Emerson was a nineteenth century American Essayist. He was also a Unitarian minister. He was a transcendentalist, what I think of as an earlier incarnation of the present-day metaphysician. Emerson said, *"Life consists of what a man is thinking all day."*

Life consists of what a man is thinking all day.

The realm of personal thought is where we find the life worth living. When we truly want to have the highest quality of life that we are capable of experiencing, then we take care with the thoughts we allow to exist in our consciousness. Our lives become the eightfold path that leads to peace of mind, and every thought we create is worthy of our Creator.

In the animal kingdom survival of the fittest reigns. For man that measure of fitness is no longer strength rooted in the physical and ruled by instinctual cunning. Now, strength is determined by will power, the capacity to make and fulfill choices that transform animal instinct into a direct grasp of Truth known as intuition. Intuitive knowledge and skill is our future. The goal is no longer survival, it is wisdom.

More than an animal

an essay first published in May 1998

By working with white whales, trainers at Sea World learned the best schedule for the animals was a mix of five basic periods each day: play, work, free time, rest, and learning time.

Upon first hearing this it might sound like something you'd like in your own life. A little bit of this, a little bit of that. After all, you need plenty of play, rest, and of course free time to balance out all your hard work and the rigorous demands of learning. You might even think you'd be a lot healthier if your boss or teacher knew about this insightful study and was willing to adjust to it.

You probably consider this idea of five periods a day a fair assessment of what a human being's balanced life might be.

It might indeed be, for an immature reasoner.

Throughout history, man has sought to understand himself through his relationship with animals. From the intricate imagery of Greek mythology to the more recent Darwinian theories of evolution by natural selection, it is commonplace for man to seek meaning by giving meaning. This is true because Man's essence is a creative spirit constantly perfecting maturation.

A beginning reasoner is one who is just beginning to consider he or she can direct the life. Such a one is beginning to separate consciousness from the outer, body shell. The greater the separation, the less he or she is subject to physical influences. The elements. The tides. Animal instincts. When the concept of how to spend time, what is important enough to spend time doing daily, dawns in the consciousness, that is the beginning of sentience. The beginning of self evaluation that leads to self awareness.

Part of the current millennium changes, a large part of

them, are influences upon the consciousness of humanity. No longer are we at this beginning of sentience, this initiation time of reasoning. In fact that happened tens of thousands of year ago, during the early stages of what is known as Atlantis.

"Does this mean we are in the adolescence of reasoning development?" one familiar with the four stages of Man might ask. And well, we might wonder, for evidence of experimentation are rampant in our world from the scientific use of animal body parts to replace damaged human ones to the psychological use of animals to elucidate, describe, and predict human behavior. Adolescence is the stage of development which births ideas like this "perfect" quintuplet schedule – where man is compared, contrasted, and subsequently reduced to an animal. Animals give man a valuable resource for reasoning and learning. It is also true that each time an animal is used to *define* Man, Man is diminished. Held back. His spiritual progress retarded. This is why so many are leaving behind the conflict of science versus religion, finding progress by blending the best both have to offer. This is most outstanding in the maturing of our ideas and practices in the area of health.

As we reach the millennium, it is time for Man to graduate to adulthood. To become accountable. This means adding to the memory built in animal man, the imagination apparent in reasoning man. Now more than ever before man is willing to embrace his own authority by moving out of the denial produced by identifying with the animal part of self and into the awareness that his thoughts are real. They have substance and energy and they determine his reality.

The reality we are now becoming aware of as we near the end of this adolescence phase is a mature sense of what we have believed all along – Man is more than a physical being. He is spirit. First. Last. Always.

The future of man does not rest in the past, in what has been, in even what is. The future of man is revealed in the imagination of the thinker. It has yet to be created. Imagination has caused every genetic change - from man's adaptability to elements to the creation of faculties for everything from fine motor skills to the tendency toward genius. In the animal kingdom survival of the fittest reigns. For man that measure of fitness is no longer strength rooted in the physical and ruled by instinctual cunning. Now, strength is determined by will power, the capacity to make and fulfill choices that transform animal instinct into a direct grasp of Truth known as intuition. Intuitive knowledge and skill is our future. The goal is no longer survival, it is wisdom. For this reason we will increasingly find Man's fittest is also the wisest among us.

So how do we make this transition? When was the last time you heard, read, or expressed the sentiment "life is for learning." An intelligent response to a youngster who just lost a big game, perhaps not so smart to say to your best friend who just lost his job, and it would be viewed as callous to say to a relative who receives a diagnosis of terminal illness. The truth of "life is for learning" remains in each instance independent of the leaner's acceptance or denial.

Like a child trusting a parent, in the infancy stage Man believes "only God (the wind, the Spirit, the sun, etc.) knows the reason." During adolescence man grapples with this because reasoning, often through science and technology, has allowed him to discover some of the answers. Sometimes he knows the reason, sometimes God does. What we do not have a reason for, we have yet to discover hence the idea *life is for learning*. Thus we add the idea of working hard to our belief in God. This becomes the way to learn, to know, to evolve through adolescence. Adulthood becomes an aligning of these two ideas. Simply stated it is doing God's will with awareness. This is the true key to a balanced life. From that wise vantage point, options become clearer. Choices easier. Fulfillment forthcoming. Health assured.

The balance we seek in our lives is not a separation of our time into various activities. The balance we seek is the capacity to respond at will. The freedom to know our lives are fulfilling a greater purpose than just using time, passing time, dividing time, spending time. The balance we seek is a command of motion, sustained and perpetually directed toward spiritual destiny. This understanding of balance is the result of living in the moment. Completely, fully, wisely. Wholistically.

To realize that play, work, free time, rest, and learning are all the same is to graduate from adolescence into adulthood. The adult knows what escapes the adolescent. These are only separate until we discover how to unite them.

As the Buddha told the crazy murderer Anguilamala, "You can kill but you cannot join, what wisdom is there in that? Even a child can destroy. Only a master can create."

That is the secret of healing. A secret we are in the process of mastering.

VI

The Spiritual Renaissance

Initiation

"The greatest discovery of my generation is that a human being can alter his life by altering his attitudes of mind."

– William James, American Psychologist (1842-1910)

Spiritual Initiation & 13 Virtues

Based upon a presentation given during the America's Secret Destiny seminar in Kansas City in the spring of 1986.

When I was young, I had the good fortune of having dedicated teachers who taught me the things necessary to know in order for me to exist in the physical world. Some of these were reading, and writing, and arithmetic. All skills needed for communication in and understanding of the world.

But I was also trained to be in the world, but not of it.

The way this transpired was through the spiritual training I received as a child. This spiritual training took the form of religion, a sect of Christianity of the Protestant bend. It would probably be best characterized as hellfire and brimstone preaching, and within it the idea of spiritual initiation was very strong. There were points in that discipline of religion that marked particular spiritual developments.

The first I experienced was days after I incarned so I have no personal memory of it, only the stories of those who were present, and a thousand or more were. The first ceremony was called a dedication to the Lord. This was where my parents brought me before the minister, in this case my evangelistic grandfather, so my soul could be consecrated in prayer and my life dedicated to a divine mission symbolized by the Lord.

As I grew older I learned that there were other rituals in our religion. One was being saved by Jesus Christ. Another was being baptized, submerged in water. There was also a ritual called speaking in tongues.

As I grew old enough to attend high school, I started meeting Catholics. I began learning about this Catholic religion which was also Christian. At the time I remember being jealous of my Catholic friends because they would tell me about their religion. They told me about ceremonies they had been going through all of their lives in conjunction with their religious beliefs. Christenings. Confirmations. Graduation ceremonies. Girls would tell me that there was a ceremony they went through around the age of 13. They would dress in beautiful white dresses to marry Jesus. My fourteen-year-old mind thought that was a pretty exciting idea. I often wondered why we didn't have something like that in our religion because the idea meant a great deal to me.

Then I heard that Catholic weddings took forever, a long time. I knew Catholic funerals were long because, as did many of my contemporaries, I had watched for days the remembrance ceremonies following the assassination of President John F. Kennedy, our first Catholic president. Through a child's eyes, I learned about spiritual initiation. I was exposed to that idea. Spirituality was very much a part of my life. The idea I had about this was that spiritual initiation is a birth of great ideas. Ideas that are spiritual in nature.

As I approached my studies in metaphysics I brought these awarenesses of spiritual initiation. My teacher in the School of Metaphysics enhanced my awareness. She taught me that there would be points of initiation in our growth and learning that would be spiritual in nature. These would be signposts, or points of accomplishment, to gauge our growth. They could also be points where we could accelerate our evolution in terms of the whole self. My ideas of spiritual initiation were embellished and enriched by what I was learning about metaphysics.

Throughout the beginning series of SOM lessons there are several points of initiation an individual experiences. Each is an expansion of consciousness that affects your everyday life, the way you treat yourself and others. They are exciting to embrace, because in doing so you expand your ability to give and to receive. You expand your awareness of who you are beyond merely the physical. You recognize there truly is a reason for some type of spiritual discipline as well as physical discipline. You begin to realize that you can gain understanding from each experience, which is indeed the purpose for being here in the material world..

As I advanced in my studies I began to realize that spiritual initiation, and the steps I was taking, were a way also to unfold what we commonly refer to in metaphysics as the assignment for a lifetime. Each individual has an appointed assignment to fulfill in their life. That assignment is not given to you by someone outside of yourself, it is given to you by your soul. Being able to be attentive to your soul once you are out here in physical activity, and being able to communicate and cooperate with that soul, you can become aware of what your assignment for being here is which adds meaning to your life.

It causes there to be a fulfillment in the choices you make. In doing so, you add to initiation a spiritual flavor. There is a person I want to talk about today who I think most of the time is not seen as a spiritual leader. I don't think if someone walked up to you and asked who are the great spiritual leaders throughout history, you would think of this person. But maybe that will change after today.

This person I think undoubtedly throughout his life, fulfilled his assignment. I hope to give you enough of a background on him that you will perhaps also draw that conclusion.

This person was very famous in literature and in our history. He was an American. The study of his life and writings conveys the idea of spiritual initiation. It does so in two ways. In spiritual initiation you have two ideas that come together to form a whole. First, *spiritual* which means that you are of spirit, you are a thinker. Then you have the idea of initiation, *to commence something, to cause something to happen.* When you bring those two together you have more than each independent of one another.

Some of the words of wisdom that this person shared through his writings I believe hold meaning for everyone because of their spiritual content. One of the things that this person is noted for saying is *"Reading makes a full man, meditation a profound man, and discourse a clear man."* Think about that. It reflects wisdom, insight borne from knowledge from both the outer and inner environments then shared with others. In few words and much detail it conveys concisely that the efficient use of our everyday waking life is to gather information, put that information together in ways that perhaps we never have before, to experience and from those experiences grow in understanding which enriches our life.

He also said, *"Wise men learn by others' harms, fools scarcely by their own."* At this point in our evolution, because we have the capability of reasoning, It is time for individuals and humanity as a whole to begin to learn not only through direct experience but also through observation. To be keenly observing of other people, how they think, the choices they make, what the results of those are.

He also said, *"How many observe Christ's birthday, how few his precepts. O tis easier to keep holidays than commandments."* I think this man had an awareness that our individual, and our combined, destiny is to become Christlike, Buddhalike, Enlightened. Franklin's clear picture captures the space between desire and manifestation. In the *Bible* this space is revealed in the words and actions of the Pharisees. The people who don't live what they preach, they are the ones who keep holidays.

He also said, *"God heals, and the doctor takes the fee."* So simple. I think this indicates this person knew something about Universal Law. He probably knew that health is not a physical matter, it doesn't start or end there. The source of health is found through spirituality or God.

He also said, *"Laziness travels so slowly that poverty soon overtakes it."* The person who wrote these words was Benjamin Franklin.

The wisdom that he built is revealed in how he lived his life. Franklin's life was very spiritual in nature. He has a list of accomplishments in the world to his credit. He lived a very full life. Franklin was born in 1706, the son of a tallow maker. By the age of 12 he was an apprentice to his brother James who was a printer. By 16 he was already the editor of a paper himself.

I've looked at great and remarkable people throughout history and I read about their lives. I think it makes sense that they would have talents and skills that they would bring into a lifetime and want to use very early. I think about that often because I work with and meet many people who have children and it's like they want to keep their kids, kids. Then I meet the child and I think, "Boy this kid needs to be stimulated. This child needs responsibility. This child needs focused adults who know how to teach the principles of concentration."

I think of this as a teacher of adults also. I see them "babying" students too. Instead of looking for their talents, skills and abilities, and stimulating them to respond to those, giving them places to be responsible for them, they are coddled, excused, and ignored. Sometimes even fixed. Benjamin Franklin, thankfully, did not have well-intended adults retard his growth.

He was already using the talents and skills his soul brought to bear upon the lifetime even before puberty.

As a result of being in the world and using it very well he was able to retire at 42. That doesn't mean he stopped.

Benjamin Franklin established many firsts. He was an initiator. He initiated the first circulating library in the colonies. He was the one who established the first hospital in the new country. He started an educational institute that became the University of Pennsylvania.

He also was used to many firsts because he was an inventor. He did experiments with the Lyden jar, and I'm sure most remember the stories about flying a kite in an electrical storm. Many of the things he discovered and brought into our realm of knowledge of electricity we now still enjoy 200 years later. All because of his efforts, what he was willing to initiate.

Franklin also invented bifocal glasses, which some of us use today. The pot bellied stove. This man had a full life, a well-rounded life.

Then of course he was politically involved. He was a diplomat, he represented our new forming country in England and France both. He was instrumental, in fact it is accredited to him, that we had a treaty with the Ohio Indians which was very important at that time. He served on the second Continental Congress and was on the committee that drafted the Declaration of Independence which set into motion this great visionary experiment of a country. He finally did die in 1790.

He lived a very full life. One thing we can say about Benjamin Franklin is that he did initiate. The word initiate actually means *to set going*. By initiating in the physical world in his dealings with people, he was able to bring to himself many experiences. The way his life unfolded it is apparent that he gained understanding from each experience. He also used that understanding to produce wisdom. I say this because of his writings. For over 40 years he published *Poor Richard's Almanac*.

One of his writings was his autobiography. In it he lists thirteen virtues. His choices cause us to realize that not only did this man initiate many things in the physical world, but he was in the world and not of it. In other words for his remarkable worldly accomplishments, he experienced many spiritual initiations as well. He was probably quite a remarkable man to know.

The list is a wonderful description of truths that apply to all of us, no matter where we live or when. His list of 13 virtues from his experience, his wisdom, went like this.

The first was temperance.

What he said about temperance was *"eat not to dullness, drink not to elevation."* Be aware of what you are doing. Reason is what separates man from all other animals.

Second virtue was silence, *"Speak not but what may benefit others and yourself. Avoid trifling conversation."* Elevate your thoughts to that which will serve the common good.

Third, order. *"Let all your things have their places, let each part of your business have its time."* A wonderful description of the Universal Law of Proper Perspective.

Fourth. Resolution. *"Resolve to perform what you ought. Perform without fail what you resolve."* Fulfilling your dharma, the duty of your soul to act in the common good.

Virtue five. Frugality. *"Make no expense but do good to others or yourself."* In other words give completely and freely from your storehouse of riches.

Six, industry. *"Lose no time, be always employed in something useful. Cut off all unnecessary passions."* Think about how your life would change if you cut out all unnecessary passions! Think how much time you'd have!

Seven, sincerity. *"Use no hurtful deceit. Think innocently and justly. And if you speak, speak ."* Speak truth as you see it. Mean what you say and say what you mean.

Eight, justice. *"Wrong none by doing injuries or omitting the benefits that are due."* Be aware of the intention behind your actions.

Nine, moderation. *"Avoid extremes, forbear resented injuries as much as you think they deserve."* Turn the other cheek by respecting people's right to their own. Strive to transcend points of view that free you to see a broader picture.

Ten, cleanliness. *"Tolerate no uncleanliness in body, clothes, or habitation."* Practice what you preach.

Eleven, tranquility. *"Be not disturbed with trifles or accidents, unavoidable."* I was talking with someone the other day who had misinterpreted a series of events and had totally fallen apart over it. She was literally out of control, beginning to believe the whole world was against her. Such a wild and unruly imagination upsets your tranquility, robbing you of peace of mind. Cultivate relaxation of body, calmness of emotion, stillness of mind.

Twelve, chastity. *"Rarely use venery but for health or offspring. Never to dullness, weakness, or the injury of your own or another's peace or reputation."* Respect the nature, power, and reason for being of the Kundalini energy. Draw upon it to create Enlightenment.

Before I tell you number thirteen, I want to share something with you. Benjamin Franklin had quite a sense of humor, and I think that is the mark of someone who knows how to go through spiritual initiations. He writes:

"My list of virtues contained at first but twelve. But a

Quaker friend, had kindly informed me that I was generally thought proud, that my pride showed itself frequently in our conversation, and that I was not content with being right when discussing a point, but was overbearing and rather insolent, of which he convinced me by mentioning several instances, I determined, endeavoring to cure myself if I could of this vice or folly among the rest, and I added humility to my list. Giving an extensive meaning to it. I cannot boast of much success in acquiring the reality of this virtue but I had a good deal with regard to the appearance of it.

"In reality there is perhaps no one of our natural passions so hard to subdue as pride. Disguise it. Struggle with it. Beat it down. Stifle it. Mortify it. As much as one pleases, it is still alive and will every now and then peep out and show itself. You will see it perhaps often in the history for even if I concede that I had completely overcome it, I should probably be proud of my ability."

It does take a good ego to go through spiritual initiations. You cannot have a small ego and do so. So be proud of your identity, of who you are. But in that pride, keep in mind Franklin's thirteen virtue: humility.

How Franklin chooses to describe this virtue, "that broad, extensive definition," is not a lot of words. He simply says, *"Imitate Jesus, and Socrates."*

If you're going to imitate Socrates, you're going to imitate one of the greatest thinkers that history remembers. You're going to imitate someone who took command of reasoning, and who used reasoning in such as way to provide a whole new structure of how to use the mind. A man who explored and created the ways and abilities to use the mind that no one else had to that point.

If you're going to imitate Jesus, you'll want to imitate the ideals and the practices that produce a Christ. These enlightening thoughts are worthy of your attention, worthy of your consideration, worthy of your time that you invest.

Imitate Jesus, and Socrates.

Through Franklin's 13 virtues, you can see he was not just accomplishing physical things. He was accomplishing wisdom, and wisdom is the mark of being able on a path to experience one spiritual initiation after another. One of his sayings, *"If you desire many things, many things will seem but a few."* You look at that and think, if I want a lot of things how can they ever seem like a few? Jesus answered this question through many parables, but like Franklin he was best when he was direct:

> *Then one of them, which was a lawyer, asked him a question, tempting him, and saying,*
>
> *Master which is the great commandment in the law?*
>
> *Jesus said unto him, "Thou shalt love the Lord thy God with all thy heart, and with all thy soul, and with all thy mind.'*
>
> *This is the first and great commandment.*
>
> *And the second is like unto it, "Thou shalt love thy neighbor as thyself."*
>
> *On these two commandments hand all the law and the prophets. (Matthew 22:35-40)*

Those who heard the teaching with only physical ears believed Jesus to be ignorant of Judaic law, the ten commandments given to the earlier Jewish leader Moses. Those who sought the spirit of Jesus' teachings found their minds and hearts opened to the universal and simple truth that is the root of all desire: love for our Creator and our fellowman.

There is such a richness in the consciousness of one who realizes Universal Truth. They insightfully know what is valuable in life and they do not hesitate to live in accordance with that knowing. They follow Jesus' counsel seeking "first the kingdom of heaven and all else" seems to come to them from the abundance of the universe as if by magic.

Life becomes very magical when you put your thoughts in order. You can discern what is truly important to you and why it is so. When what you value is rooted not in things that are transient, things that are physical, but rather what is spiritual in nature, you find your life truly is simple. You may have many desires, but they really are very few. In order to embark upon spiritual initiations you must desire wisdom and knowledge.

It is important to initiate change. To initiate in the physical. To make things happen. But it must be mindful. The spiritually aware do so to cause motion, to cause learning, to cause wisdom to flourish in the self. When you cause it, you are an Initiate. You move yourself to inner depths and you eventually create mastery in your existence.

I believe it is possible for everyone to attain such mastery.

I believe each of us have the capability to be remembered as Benjamin Franklin is. We have the capacity to initiate many things in the physical and to grow spiritually. Consider what you want to do with your life. Consider what you've done already and consider what you are capable of doing from this day forward. Endeavor to make your life a series of spiritual initiations that will culminate in your mastery of your whole self.

Come into light. Realize the power of creation, the reality of God, every day in every thought.

The answer is simple. Instead of engaging in intellectual arguments, we can agree — unanimously — to foster the genius within our children. To encourage their natural inclination for learning and their love for the Truth. To serve as examples of good will and spiritual advancement by offering the best of who we are.

A Different World

an essay first published in 1997

At first thought, the topic of Internet "censorship" may seem incongruous to an issue on health and healing. However upon investigation and reflection, I have found the subject illuminates the quality of thinking that can produce a miraculous healing in ourselves as individuals, as a society, and as a planet.

The Internet is the information superhighway. It is the world's neighborhood library. Just like the pictures the commercials paint, whether you are a Buddhist monk in the Himalayas or a sailor on a boat in the Pacific, if you have a personal computer, telephone service, and a company that can access the Internet then you have the "vehicle" needed to travel on that "highway." Whether you are two, twenty, or one hundred and twenty you can access information on everything from religious doctrine to medical research, from the world's greatest art treasures to the latest sports scores. For anyone hungry for information, the Internet is a dream come true.

However, the Internet is becoming much more than the neighborhood library. It is the neighborhood school, basketball arena, movie theater, travel bureau, and even pornography shop. I have been told there are seamy establishments being constructed daily on this new highway, not only pornography, but websites illustrating all means and executions of man's inhumanity to his fellow man.

This creates a dilemma.

Where the written word requires education for comprehension and imagination for experience, the electronic nature of the Internet needs neither. Its user requirements are physical: equipment, prearranged access, and the ability to push buttons. Some Internet sites reportedly include scenes beyond the imagination of most of us; the kinds of horrors faced by war veterans or law enforcement agents or fire fighters; horrors they keep to themselves not wanting to disrupt the gentler, more peaceful consciousness of home.

The question being raised is: "Do we as a society need to ensure that the material available on the Internet is suitable for children?"

The answer became quite clear to me when I heard one man, a lawyer, disdainfully say, "The issue is do we want to reduce what adults can see to the level of a child? That would be a different world."

I pondered his statement for many days.

And I had to agree, it would be a very different world. In fact, the more I contemplated it, the more I meditated on it, I realized that that is exactly the kind of world we could all embrace!

Idealistically, every parent wants the best for his or her children. We want smarter teachers, kinder neighbors, cleaner environments, safer streets; a better world for our children to live in. We want a bright future, filled with not just freedom from any pain we have known, but with opportunity for a fulfilling life. A future of hope and of promise. Such a future begins today in the minds of people like you and I.

The answer is simple. Instead of engaging in intellectual arguments, we can agree – unanimously – to foster the genius within our children. To encourage their natural inclination for learning, and their love for the Truth. To serve as examples of good will and spiritual advancement by offering the best of who we are. For some there seems to be a time as they moved from childhood toward adulthood this sense of best was spoiled. They believe this happens to everyone. It's as if suddenly they became too jaded to be kind, too sophisticated to trust, too cynical to dream, to angry too understand, too greedy to be generous. If this is so therein lies the seed of illness in ourselves and our society. And the rest of us must do what we can to create a different world for us all.

In this country, there are those who claim the First Amendment to the U.S. Constitution, the amendment guaranteeing freedom of speech, will be violated if there are regulations and, yes restrictions, on what people can publicly do. The key is publicly. Plato once commented, "Until philosophers are kings, or the kings and princes of this world have the spirit and power of philosophers, and political greatness and wisdom meet in one, and those commoner natures who pursue either to the exclusion of the other one compelled to stand aside, cities will never rest from their evils." The greatest use of government is to encourage common standards of responsible conduct in the liberties we enjoy with our fellow man. Personal integrity, public accountability.

Currently the images, sounds, and increasingly the interaction available via the Internet are a manifestation of neither. This was not always the case. The Internet began with principles and ideals, a merging of government and higher education. However with the advent of availability reaching the masses, those principles and ideals are no longer commonly accepted. Now, the Internet has a virulent streak, reflecting the chaos that results when there is freedom without responsibility. The dilemma this proposes reminds me of the symbol of American jurisprudence, the blindfolded woman holding the scales of justice. If we insist on remaining blind as a society to the disease-producing elements within and among ourselves will we want to live in the world it creates?

Eyes are meant to be used. The Internet electronically disseminates information without consideration of the qualifications or intentions of the source. This is the true concern that must be addressed: do we want to live with the effects of a technological world void of human intelligence and wisdom. Standards are not a matter of censorship, they are a means of establishing guidelines, an attempt to insure personal integrity and public accountability for the common good. An expression of the desire for a better world.

Where the valiant qualities illustrated in every classical children's story - indeed every Holy scripture - of the world are held in high esteem as ideals to strive for the world is a better place to live. As Confucius stated 2500 years ago, "To put the world in order, you must first put the nation in order. To put the nation in order, you must first put the family in order. To put the family in order, you must first put your personal self right. You must set your heart aright." Personal integrity, public accountability.

Another master teacher, Jesus of Nazareth, encouraged spiritual seekers to "Come as little children". Curious. Open-minded. Truthful. Eager. Willing. I believe as we endeavor to make a world fit for children, we will create a world fit for all of us. A spiritually uplifting and morally sound world, free of disease.

As the man said, a different world.

VII

The Spiritual Renaissance

Awareness

"Great men are they
who see that the Spiritual
is stronger than any material force;
that thoughts rule the world."

–Ralph Waldo Emerson, American poet & essayist (1803-1882)

Spiritual Awareness

The Second Coming of Christ

Based upon an Interfaith sermon given during the 17th annual SOM Camp Out, July of 1989.

If the Christ returned and he was of a race different than your own would you follow him?

If the Christ returned and he was a communist, or from a country foreign to your own, would you follow him?

If the Christ returned and he was physically impaired, or perhaps even a clone, the result of science would you follow him?

Now, think about your best friend. Go beyond what he or she looks like, the interests and talents, the reasons that make you friends. Think with your mind, and with your heart. Now, what if the Christ returned as that person sitting next to you, would you follow?

When I have asked these questions, the responses are much more revealing than the questions themselves. Most people have never considered the possibility that Christ can walk in their midst let alone be someone they love. The change in thinking that will lead us to embrace the principle of cosmic consciousness personified in the Christ is part of our Spiritual Renaissance.

Everywhere in humanity there is evidence that individuals, through their appointed or chosen religions, are looking for a Christ figure. The word Christ is usually associated only with the religion that bears its name – Christianity. Yet when we go below the surface, we find that the word Christ, comes from the Greek word *christos* which means anointed or enlightened one. Christ is a title, like doctor or sir in current society. When I first realized Christ was not Jesus' last name but rather a religious title of respect and admiration a new realm of understanding opened before me. Christ began to symbolize a divine state worthy of my aspiration. Much more than doctor, denoting scientific learning and aptitude, or sir, recognizing the accomplishments of age, Christ symbolized an advancement in consciousness rarely seen upon the face of the earth.

Because I was raised with Christian beliefs, the concept of Christians looking for the second coming of Christ was familiar to me. Christians believe the Christ came once to the earth and is going to return. As I grew older I learned this concept is shared around the world, for it exists in religious traditions everywhere. The Jews are looking for a Messiah. The Muslims are looking for the Makti. The Buddhists are looking for the Buddha. This was an amazing point of interconnectedness for me.

In any of the world's major religions we find that human man – according to his own beliefs, his own understanding of his essence, of who he is and of his relationship to God – is looking for something. That something is a savior. The "savior" is described with many different words. Over the years, I have made friends with people of different religious faiths. Our talks have taught me that when we go beyond the words, the labels, we discover compatible hopes, desires, and beliefs. We all believe in a savior that will in some way lead mankind into the light of greater understanding. No one religion has cornered the market on this expectation that there will be a savior however there was a time you could not have convinced me of it.

When I was growing up I used to think that Christ was Jesus' last name. Every time someone referred to Jesus they would say Jesus Christ. It would be as an adult reading the Biblical text that

I would finally learn his name: Jesus of Nazareth, Nazareth being the place he lived when he was young. In the time and place of his existence, people were identified according to their family. Where the family came from was important. If you are familiar with the birth of Christ account in the *Bible* then you probably know that Jesus was born in Bethlehem. He was of the house of David, the *Old Testament* boy who slew Goliath and earned a kingdom. Lineage was very important to the Jewish people symbolically because our common Source is very important to all of humanity.

The *New Testament* of the *Bible*, where Jesus' story is told, was written by several people two thousand years ago. Just as modern novelists build their stories on people they have known through their lives, these authors used the people, places, and things of their time to tell a story, to paint a picture. The difference between a good novelists and one who pens a Holy work is more than the source of the material. Holy works are written in the Universal Language of Mind. They are books concerned with the evolution of mankind. I personally think that the *Bible* has a great deal of truth to offer anyone because in the Universal Language of Mind it contains Universal Laws and Universal Truths and instruction in those Universal Laws and Truths.

This language of the spirit can be taught and learned, as can more physical means of communicating like English or Spanish. The beauty is, even if you've never studied the language, anyone can gain insight by reading Holy works because they are spiritual in nature. "*For those with eyes to see it,*" as Jesus was fond of saying. Those "eyes to see" come from the mind and they come from the heart of the individual. They don't come from the body. The availability of all Holy works is a privilege at this point in our evolution. They give us instruction for developing the spiritual eye so we are able to see Christ in action.

I don't know what your thoughts were when asked to

consider Christ as a Caucasian, Negroid, or Mongoloid; or as a communist, an invalid or a product of science. I don't know what your thoughts were, but you do. I do know when I have presented these thoughts to groups I've heard some chuckles and even a few gasps. I've seen some uncomfortable shifting in seats and I've seen slow, knowing smiles spread across people's faces. The thoughts that reflect in our responses are not new. In fact, if we go back and examine what was occurring at the day and time when Jesus arrived, and some of the attitudes of the people around him who he taught, I think we will begin to unravel some of our own thinking.

During the time that the man Jesus was alive there were three major sects in the Hebrew religion. One was called the Sadducees, references to them appear in the gospels, the *New Testament* accounts of Jesus' life. The Sadducees were devoted to the Pentateuch, the writings which comprise the first five books of the *Old Testament* in the *Bible*. These are the books of Moses, one of the great Hebrew leaders, to whom God gave the divine law. Although dedicated to the rule of law, and perhaps because of this dedication, Sadducees were very materialistic in the way that they approached things. They did not believe in the resurrection.

A second sect was known as the Pharisees. The Pharisees recognized the Pentateuch as well but they more importantly recognized as a complete expression of divine law what is called the Talmud. The Talmud is oral law in Jewish tradition. It is passed on by word of mouth. The Pharisees immersed themselves in talking about the law and how to live. They lived by the letter of the law, and were very concerned with being able to follow what was laid out in those laws as they saw it.

The third sect was called the Essenes. The Essenes are not widely recognized primarily because the Bibles handed down to us do not mention them. Editors through the years have deleted those references. Even so, knowledge of their existence and beliefs is available. The Essenes were an important sect of Hebrew people at the time of the birth of Jesus. The Essenes were very concerned with spiritual knowledge; what could be attained and what could be gained by an individual. They were very active in the pursuit of producing a Messiah. They knew that a Messiah or a savior was to come and they wanted to prepare themselves to receive that coming. Their activity, their appointed duty, was to copy and to recopy the book of Isaiah. Remember this was two thousand years ago. There are no Xerox machines or computers. There are only reeds or feathers from animals, and dyes made from plants available for the task. The goal in the mind of every Essene was for every Jew to have a copy of this book of prophecy. As a result the Essenes were invested in prophecy and the fulfillment of prophecy.

It was from the sect of the Essenes that Jesus was born.

Let's begin with the Sadducees, exploring what this group of people might be symbolically teaching us about ourselves. The books of the Bible are divided into chapters which sometimes are semi-divided into sections denoting trains of thought or a change in the location or action. In *Matthew* 22:23 the subheading "*Saddducees and the Resurrection.*" appears.

"That same day some Sadducees who hold that there is no resurrection, came to him with a question."

Now you have to realize Jesus has returned to the land area of his birth and has been teaching his own people for several years. He is teaching whoever will listen. He has just gotten a point across to *"render unto Caesar what is Caesars and unto God what is God's."* In the metaphysical interpretation, the Universal Language of Mind, this means to be able to separate the physical, material world from the mental, spiritual existence. It is the wisdom that gives each the value and credence they deserve, realizing their purposes are uniquely different.

> *"That same day some Sadducees who hold that there is no resurrection came to him with a question. Teacher, Moses declared if a man dies without children his brother must take the wife and produce offspring for his brother. Once there were seven brothers the eldest died after marrying and since he had no children left his wife to his brother, the same thing happened to the second, the third and so on down to the seventh. Last of all the woman died too. At the resurrection whose wife will she be since all seven of them married her?"*

Now this is typical of the type of questioning that's produced from a "Sadducees" mind. It reminds me very much of a question I used to ask my parents and my minister. I was raised to look at the *Bible* in a somewhat spiritual way but the basis of what I was taught was literal, physically-based because I was not taught a structure like the language of mind to understand its universal meaning. One of my early questions concerned Adam and Eve, the first two people named in the *Bible*. I always wondered where the wives for Adam and Eve's sons came from. If they came from Adam and Eve that would mean incest which I had learned was wrong.

It was not to embarrass someone that I would ask this type of question. I really wanted to understand. I saw enough value in this book, enough truth, that I knew if there were other things I did not understand then the lacking was in me. The lacking was in my ability to understand and identify the truth, and I was willing to learn, to change, in order to grow in that understanding. So in the beginning of my seeking answers, in what I would call my "Sadducee period", I asked questions very similar to this very physical question noted in *Matthew*. See to be a "Sadducee", to have that kind of mental condition, is not bad. But it does indicate a certain frame of mind, that is highly limiting, to the individual. It indicates a kind of physical thinking only, that leaves you with many questions that are not answerable in the material world.

To understand this Biblical passage, we need to read Jesus' reply to this question. He said,

> *"You are badly misled, because you fail to understand the scriptures and the power of God. When people rise from the dead they neither marry nor are given in marriage, but live like angels in heaven."*

Remember the Sadducees held that there was no resurrection. A Biblical scholar will take the time to research the origins of words used in the *Bible* or in any holy work. So a Biblical scholar will know that the word *resurrection* comes from a Latin word *resurrectio* meaning to rise again. The Sadducees are asking Jesus to comment on what we would now describe as life and death. They want to know about one of the eternal questions of mankind. What's going to happen after this lifetime is over? They don't believe that there is anything more and their belief leaves room for doubt. So they want to know the thoughts of this teacher whose reputation has spread throughout the Hebrew people. Jesus' reply is that "you are misled", there is something lacking in the understanding. It's very much like my young understanding of Adam and Eve. I knew there was something else for me to understand. Jesus even tells the Sadducees what is missing: admitting the divine capacity of thought to create.

Jesus instructs the Sadducees that life continues to exist. We change form when the body dies. *"You neither marry nor are given in marriage."* Existence is not the same as it is out here in the material world. *"You live like angels in heaven"*, we are spirit.

When you begin to explore the inner workings of your mind learning how to move in the inner levels of consciousness, the body you use for inner level travel is not the physical body of your waking hours. Rather it is akin to the body you use in your dreams. Walking and talking in this etheric body is known as astral projection. In astral projection you begin to visit the inner worlds of existence. You realize that you do indeed exist as a being apart from your physical body and your five physical senses. This is what Jesus is trying to get across to the Sadducees.

He goes on to instruct them further as to the fact that the dead are raised:

> *"Have you not read what God said to you 'I am the God of Abraham, the God of Jacob, the God of Isaac.' He is the God of the living, not of the dead. The crowds who listened were spellbound by his teaching."*

In the language of mind as we explore and study the *Bible* we find that the *"I am"* symbolizes true individuality, the essence that knows who we are, where we came from, and where we are to go. By studying the *Old Testament*, we find that *Abraham* is talking about the conscious mind, his offspring *Isaac*, the subconscious mind, and his offspring *Jacob*, the superconscious mind. When you have awareness of yourself beyond just the physical you have experience with the truth being taught here by Jesus. When you are no longer a slave or a victim to physical-thinking only, your ideas of life change. You begin to see beyond physical birth and physical death. Like watching the cycles of seasons or the growing of a tree from a seed, existence unfolds itself as a continuity of birth, life, death, and resurrection. You begin to see that all that really happens is that we change forms.

One of the services the School of Metaphysics provides is intuitive reporting. I am one of the reporters. One of the reports is a Crossing of Paths that researches where and when two individuals were associated in a prior lifetime and how that experience is impacting the present day relationship. It reveals the karmic obligation. Sometimes people want to know if the other person is their soul mate. Most of the time, they want to know what they can do to aid the other person. They feel a sense of responsibility, an indebtedness, to this individual.

This is very much the same type of thinking that is being described in the passage. After all a man who had seven brothers was married. He died. His next brother took the wife, then he died. Then the next brother did the same all the way down the line so the woman ended up having seven different husbands at seven different times. The Sadducee question is "Okay, who is she going to be married to later on? if there is a resurrection?" The Sadducees don't even believe there *is* a resurrection. This reminds me of the questions some people ask during intuitive reports. They are more interested in whether they were married in a past life than in the insight provided by the research into their present life. If the report does not meet their expectations, they pay no attention to it, missing the wealth that exists now in their life. Sometimes, like the Sadducees people who believe the current life to be the only one of its kind, a person requests a past life profile "just because I'm curious." Curiosity is the beginning of knowledge, and knowledge can be a forerunner of wisdom.

Jesus tried to point the Sadduccees of his time in that direction by urging them to look within for answers. Intuitive reports do the same.

The Sadducee type of thinking will limit you. It is only a place to start; a place to question, to look beyond.

Then we have the Pharisees. In the next chapter of Matthew, number 23, we have a passage called *"The Hypocrisy of the Scribes and Pharisees."* Hypocrisy is from a Greek word meaning "to feign discernment." In other words you're faking it. You are pretending that you know how to separate and identify what you see. You're bluffing that you are able to reason. You're faking that you know what makes sense or what is truth for you. Feigning discernment is a characteristic of the scribes and the Pharisees. Whenever Jesus wants to teach the Pharisees this is the type of thing that he says:

> *"Then Jesus told the crowds and his disciples, 'The scribes and the Pharisees have succeeded Moses as teachers. Therefore do everything, and observe everything, they tell you.'*

This gives them a place of importance. Remember, the Pharisees lived *by the letter* of the law. They were very attached to the dictates of the law. So it makes sense to me that Jesus would instruct us to do everything and observe everything that they would tell you. However these truths are often distorted in delivery or reception. They are the "supposed to's" and "should's" that we hear in our heads. One of those should's that I was raised with is "you should go to church on Sunday and when you are there you should stay awake and you should pay attention." For a number of years the truth of this was lost on me because I saw it in a two-dimensional sense, someone trying to tell me what to do, trying to force their ideas on me. I was in a Pharisee frame of mind, battling the letter of the law in search of the spirit and missing the value of both.

Jesus goes on: *"But do not follow their example."*

What a shocker that is. You are going to do everything that someone tells you to do, but you are not going to follow their example! How many years was I in a spiritual wasteland because

I blamed the hypocrisy of people in my own religion? How long did it take me to heed this wise counsel to separate the messenger from the message? All the while the answer was here, Jesus says not to follow the example of the Pharisees because: *"Their words are bold, but their deeds are few."*

Have you ever met somebody like this? They can enthrall with rhetoric, inspire with lofty images, but you look at their life and their life doesn't match the words they are saying at all. So many times people become caught up in appearances, what things look like, and miss the essence where there is truth. Jesus repeatedly said his kingdom was in Heaven not of earth. The Truth is only as meaningful as it is given life by its perceiver. Perhaps there are truths you preach but don't practice. Most parents have them. The "do as I say, not as I do" teaching method. This is Pharisee consciousness.

Jesus goes on: *"They bind up heavy loads hard to carry, to lay on other men's shoulders, while they themselves will not lift a finger to budge them."* These are the kind of thoughts, "somebody really ought to do something."

> *"All their works are preformed to be seen. They widen their phalactries and wear huge tassels. They need an audience. They are fond of places of honor at banquets and the front seats in synagogues, of marks of respect in public, and being called rabbi. As to you, avoid the title rabbi. One among you is your teacher, the rest are learners. Do not call anyone on earth your father, only one is your father, the one in heaven."*

Many people have read this to mean that *only* one among you is your teacher and the rest among you are learners, that the *Bible* says there has only been one person who illustrated the Christ principle. But is that true? If that is not quite true, then what is the truth? Jesus tells them *"do not call any one on earth your father."* If we interpret this physically Jesus is encouraging us to lie, wouldn't you say? Everyone has a physical mother and father. To deny that, to refuse to admit it, saying "I don't have a father," would mean that you are lying. Is that what Jesus is saying? *"Only one is your father the one in heaven."* Are we to listen to no one? "Only one is your teacher, the Messiah." Are we to worship the dead, or passively wait for the future?

What do you think Jesus was really saying? Put yourself back two thousand years ago. You're in the audience and Jesus is saying this to you. What are you thinking? What is he doing breaking his arm patting himself on his back saying he is the Messiah? That he is the only one here to teach? I don't think so. I don't think so. Listen:

> *"The greatest among you will be the one who serves the rest. Whoever exalts himself shall be humbled, but whoever humbles himself shall be exalted."*

As do increasing numbers of people, I devote my time to many voluntary pursuits. I am joined by others throughout the country who volunteer their talents and skills as well as their time for the betterment of others. Some of us serve food, some give the gift of reading, some clean and repair, some are just willing to be there for someone to trust. Since the School of Metaphysics is a voluntary organization, where financial reward is never a measure of personal investment, I have been witness to astounding communities of people serving others. One of the things I have learned is the Truth that within every person is a sincere, real desire to give. I have seen people jump right in over and over, serving the rest. This behavior is guided by a type of thinking in action that brings this passage alive for you. As you voluntarily serve, you become acquainted with your inner teacher. There is only one inner teacher, the storehouse of wisdom which is the subconscious mind within each of us. There is only one "saviour" or "messiah" that you have. Only one "I Am" within. The way you come to know these inner parts of Self is to be of service to others. Be willing to open your eyes, to look and to see. To see something that needs to be done, to respond thereby aiding someone else is to move beyond the mind of the Pharisee. "Do not follow the example of the Pharisees" because all they give is lip service. They are smooth talkers, but watch what they do.

To understand Pharisee consciousness, I encourage people to think before acting, and to make certain their thoughts and words match. It is essential for enlightenment that what we are saying is the same as what we are thinking. When you wouldn't dare say what you are thinking, that's a perfect time to do some serious attitude adjusting. If you feel badly about the thoughts you think that is a stimulus for you to change the way you think. Aligning thoughts and actions is one of the best cures I know to an illness that is produced when someone is immersed in Pharisee consciousness. This consciousness is a stage we experience whenever we are learning. It is the place where we are thinking half-spiritually and half-physically. Some of the answers make sense and we can see true cause, and some are beyond us so, failing to perceive cause, we blame others. Sometimes we are in control of our lives, sometimes we are victims. That's the Pharisee condition of mind.

Reading about Jesus' teaching and healing ministry is the best example of the consciousness symbolized by the Essenes. From research I have studied I believe Jesus, the seeker, travelled extensively, adding to his experience and wisdom. I don't think that he blinded himself to what had been nor did he turn away from truth wherever he happened to find it. I think he investigated it. I think he actively searched for it. Just as you and I are. In that searching, in that discovering and building of awareness, is how he earned his title of Christ.

I told you that Christ is from a Greek word *Christos* meaning enlightened or anointed one. From a metaphysical point of view of understanding the inner levels of mind, "Christhood" can be interpreted. Your own Christhood, your own inner plan to evolve and develop, is held in what we teach as the first level of consciousness. This is the most inward level of mind. The beginning of the mind as it expresses from its Source. The Christ awareness exists within each individual, look for it. Salute it when you see it. It is there. Do not be distracted by outward things, by how people look, by how they sound. Actively look for that part because you will develop the eyes to see and that will aid you in bringing out the Christ in you.

Christians believe that Christ has come once and he is going to come again. I agree with that, because I do adhere to the teachings of Jesus that tell us how to live as a Christ. The first coming was in our awareness, Light's desire to mature, and in the development of mind. The pushing out from the Source into individual expression. The second coming is at hand for each one of us. That second coming is when we take the time, the energy, the will, the desire required to move inward. To recapture, at last with awareness and maturity, our own Christhood.

There was a man who came to Jesus at one point. He was a young man, saying, *"Master I want to know how to get to heaven."* Jesus, as with any spiritual teacher you will find, was very pleased to accept a question and offer guidance. He said, *"If you are to reach heaven you need to follow the commandments."* These are the ten commandments given to Moses. *"I am the Lord thy God," "Honor thy Father and thy Mother," "Thou shalt not kill," "Thou shalt not commit adultery,"* and so forth. The young man replied, well I've kept those since I was a young boy, I've done that. What else do I need to do? And Jesus replied,

> *'Go away and sell all your possessions and give the money to the poor.' And the young man was very dejected and he turned away and walked away."*

In these dawning days of Spiritual Renaissance I think sometimes we don't know the answer to "When the Christ returns will we follow him?" because we become distracted by earthly things, by momentary things in our own experience, that we know will pass. They are not going to last forever but we still hold onto them. We still hold onto people and places and things, tenaciously, even to the point of "killing" them. Allowing to the type of thinking described here. Do not be as the young man, do not turn away from the truth. When your spirit is tried meet the test. Only a creator is wise enough to know that anything he has he can recreate at will. This is freedom.

Where is this expanded consciousness that knows freedom? It is inside where the spirit resides. Evaluate what you hold holy in your life. Seek the meaning for your existence and allow it to touch every moment of your day.

We know about the great masters of our world because Holy scriptures were written by their contemporaries. Whether it is the Christ that you're seeking, or the Makti, or the Messiah, look to what that one embodies. Seek to know His essence for the name does not matter. What does matter is what that idea stimulates in you. What we can find in the teachings of Jesus, or the teachings of Zarathustra, or the teachings of Gautama, or the teachings of Quetzecotal, are the ways to achieve illumined awareness. The means to become enlightened.

This question that we began with is not really a question

outside of you. It is a question that each man must answer within his own soul. When you know this answer another question will arise.

When the Christ appears, will you be too busy with earthly things, with things that are temporary, to heed the call? Or will you be one of the individuals who follow the teaching of one of these great masters in order to earn the title of an Enlightened One?

What became overwhelmingly apparent to me as the day of her funeral approached was how a death became an event that impressed the consciousness of the world.

The fact that much of the world was united by grief for a woman they never met is remarkable. It speaks to our capacity to embrace strangers.

Cinderella's Death

It was growing late. I was preparing to go upstairs to put our two-and-a-half year old to bed when my husband told me CNN was reporting that something had happened to Princess Diana.

I lingered. Just having read yet another account of her life, this one on how she had recently fallen in love, I immediately felt anxious. The first news was sketchy as it unfolded. A car crash in a Parisian tunnel. Motorcycles. An explosion, screeching, a crash. Four people, two dead. The princess was taken to a local hospital. I found myself saying a special prayer for the lady I'd never met.

Little more than an hour later, after my son was peacefully sleeping, I joined my husband who told me Princess Diana had died. I was saddened. I continued to watch the sparse reports for a while, as if, should I watch long enough, someone would come on to say it had all been a mistake. But no one ever did

The next day I was vaguely distracted. I could concentrate on the things at hand but my attention kept coming back to the death of a woman younger than myself. Why her? Why now? Being a metaphysician I knew there were lines of karmic obligation, personal to those involved, which elevate death from the level of cruel misfortune to the soul's destiny. What those debts might have been quickly became apparent. By the next morning Princess Diana's image was everywhere. Modern media consumed her in death, as it had in life. Television for the most part treated her respectfully, as more than just another story. Throughout the week period from her death in France to her funeral in England, newspapers and magazines, all the public avenues of communication were filled with memories of her life and speculation on her life's impact. From whether she was mistreated by the royal family to her sons to the possible influence her death might have on the global meeting to discuss banning land mines, speculation and opinion were plentiful. Media, trying to distance itself from the photographers who hounded the Princess, was arrogantly ironic in its newly found objectivity, unrepentent in its culpability, and remiss in its indictments of what needs to change in us all.

The truth is the day Diana Spencer chose to marry Charles, the Prince of Wales, she also chose to become the manifestation of a dream. Diana was a living fairy tale, a real princess that because of mass communication we all knew. Millions of us attended her wedding even if we never received a personal invitation. It was her marriage that catapulted her into the limelight of public attention. It was her own personal charisma that kept her there even when the fairy tale threatened to end with her divorce.

Women were captivated by this youthful nanny who became the mother of a future king. This pretty girl filled with insecurities which fueled the self-destruction of bulimia. This girl who became a stunning woman, the most photographed woman in the world. A woman who overcame a problem shared by many young women. A woman who increased her prestige and fortune through marriage and created her own niche of importance by dedicating time to causes she deemed worthy of her attention. She embodied the emancipation of all women.

Diana was a myth come alive. The day she chose to marry she left behind her privacy, her upperclass normalcy, and entered into the realm of celebrity. Her conflict and pain stemmed from fighting the responsibility of her own choices. In some unconscious way, many identified with that part of her humaneness. Even those who had never been interested in the Princess when she was alive, now found themselves having some opinion upon hearing of her death.

She became a modern day human sacrifice. When she became a celebrity, she lost her old life. She had to fashion a new one. She never seemed to understand why but she knew there was no place of obscurity for her so she learned to use celebrity to help others. She held hands with AIDS patients before it was known to be safe. She comforted the abused. She traveled to areas of the world where land mines still rob people of their freedom, their limbs, their lives. Like a modern day Pandora, she was the "accessible" member of a royal family.

Somehow we, even the males among us, personalized this woman. She was the girl next door who went farther than we ever thought possible. She was the one who lived on the other side of town, the one who always got her picture in the paper. She was the woman we fantasied being or marrying. We saw her as the woman who was wronged, not as the adulterer. We saw her as the underdog, not as a modern-day Mordred. We were willing to forgive her, as if doing so would make us better people. She was like the old friend whom we no longer see but like to hear about. We could rejoice at the birth of her children and now we would cry at her early death.

And when all is said and done it was probably the timing of her demise that arrested our collective attention. Those of the same age were confronted with their own mortality, death can come at any moment. Those younger lost an idol or a heroine, a dream that ended prematurely. Those older ponder the capricious fortune that takes such a beautiful girl from us too soon. What became overwhelmingly apparent to me as the day of her funeral approached was how a death became an event that impressed the consciousness of the world.

The fact that much of the world was united by grief for a woman they never met is remarkable. It speaks to our capacity to embrace strangers. Sometime between 1982 and 1997 Diana ceased being a woman, mother, princess, and became a universal symbol for us. An archetypal symbol of what most people in the Western world value as desirable: wealth, power, family, fame. Perhaps that is why it was so easy for the people who shape what we collectively think, the communicators, the media, to be captivated by her. It was the media who made her life an open book so we all might have a contemporary myth of love and betrayal, banishment and redemption. And so it was how the media wrote the story that shaped our ideas. Like the oral delivery of storytellers in another time and place, the images we saw of Diana during that week enabled us to learn the story well.

It would be the passing of another woman, twice Diana's age and half a world away, who would place the Princess's death in perspective.

Like a divine hand sweeping over the Earth, news of Mother Teresa's death came on the eve of Diana's well planned and much anticipated funeral. The media review of Mother's life was sparse, as if the visual images she left behind of poverty and death are too painful for us to bear. But in the few pictures commonly broadcast the contrast between the two women was obvious.

Mother was the epitome of humbleness, to her everyone was valued and special. Everyone was a child of God. Without question she believed those who were more fortunate should help others. When reporters would want to interview her she would not sit in a studio or some other comfortable place of luxury. Rather she would invite them to come with her as she made her rounds. She did more than introduce reporters to her world, she included them often handing reporters an infant to hold. Her belief that everyone who can should respond to the needy pricked at the conscience. The way she thought and the way she lived was always inspiring, the imaginations were fueled into transcendent realms or propelled into self-repudiation and chastisement.

The strength of her altruistic belief proved to be a bitter pill for many who lead comfortable lives, being generous with their money to pay someone else to do what they will not thereby refusing to give what is most valuable–themselves. It was this reality more than the lack of glamour or royalty or myth that kept knowledge of Mother Teresa away from us. The awareness of those who make the decisions of what will be broadcast into all our lives is more attracted by the secular, physicalness of life than the religious, spirituality of it. This is a testimony to the height of Human Man, that bridge of consciousness connecting Reasoning Man with Intuitive Man. And the way Mother Teresa's death was portrayed by the same media who covered Diana's illustrates the beginning of Human Man's decline.

In many ways there is a greater symbolic progression here. Diana, the flawed princess but triumphant woman, easily symbolizes the struggle of mankind to wield reasoning, the awareness of what is right and what is wrong and the sagacity to choose the former. Diana was very human. Her consciousness matured, reaching to make something of herself, her life, and she found her calling at first from her own weaknesses. In her final years she would grow enough to develop sympathy for individuals into compassion for humanity. This was well demonstrated by her choice in the last year of her life to use her high visibility to spotlight the inhumanity of the political neglect that allows land mines to continue to maim men, women, and children. Diana epitomized how truly wealthy we all are, how we can misplace our sense of worth by valuing what is temporary, and through trial and error like a Prodigal Son return with understanding borne from experience. She symbolized Human Man's tendency to learn the hard way.

Ironically, most people would believe Mother Teresa's life to be the harder of the two. The poor living conditions, with few if any modern conveniences we in the West have come to take for granted, the constant emotional climate of disease and death. Most people in the West spend their lives running from the realities of life so they marvel at someone like Mother Teresa. No doubt it is easier for most to imagine themselves being served dinner at Buckingham Palace than envisioning themselves an angel of mercy to a ten pound two-year-old in a Calcutta gutter. With this in mind the difference becomes more apparent. Mother Teresa lived a life of service, dedicating her life to care for the poorest of the poor. She did not just visit the poor and suffering and dying. She lived with them.

At 18, younger than when Diana married her prince, Agnes Gonxha Bojaxjiu moved from Macedonia to Calcutta to join a Roman Catholic order in the midst of Hindu India.

Because of her deeds, others recognized her as "Mother Teresa." She was known but not a celebrity. She chose God, and her choice affected the world. She spoke of doing God's work, and said that the dying were "Jesus in distressing disguise."

Diana was a public figure, a celebrity on the cover of magazines, a newsmaker. She chose marriage. She did man's work.

Both tried to use life to do good.

Mother Teresa was admired because she embodied who we can always chose to be but rarely do. Diana was admired because she embodied who we pretend to be and in large measure who we are.

In the end the moral of their lives may best be described in clothing. Diana used what came her way, apparel from those the world describes as fashion designers, the ones who command large sums of money for what they do with needles and materials and imagination. She looked like a Barbie doll, tailored suit with hat and shoes or evening dress with jewels. She looked like she stepped out of a magazine and there she often appeared. Just months before her death, it is said at her son's urging, Diana gave several of her designer gowns to be auctioned.

As for Mother Teresa she wore the same type of sari day in and day out for fifty years. When she died it is said she owned two of them, along with a pair of shoes, and a rosary.

It is not a question of which woman was greater.

Their deaths just days apart are much more significant than such egotistical fancy. Egos aside, I believe of the two, Mother Teresa will be remembered for centuries to come. It is she who will be immortalized in man's world as a saint. Her legend will live on.

She lived very much in the world without ever being of it and in so doing brought a light to the world, a light carried on by thousands who were inspired by her goodness "to be like."

VIII

The Spiritual Renaissance

Transformation

"When a nation makes progress
in science, technology, economic life,
and the prosperity of its citizens,
a great contribution is made to civilization.
But all should realize that these things
are not the highest good,
but only instruments for pursuing such goods."

– Pope John XXIII, leader of Catholic Church, (1881-1963)

"The life given us by nature is short,
but the memory of a well-spent life is eternal."

– Marcus Tullius Cicero, Roman orator (106-43 BC)

Spiritual Transformation
Being in the World

Based upon a talk entitled ""Summoning a Nation"
given during the annual SOM Teachers Conference in July, 1991..

Man craves days, hours, minutes filled with experiences. We fill our lives with what we believe to be important. Please take a moment to think about what is important to you.

Go to your favorite place and fill your mind with thoughts of what makes life valuable for you. Think deeply. Take all the time you need, and want. Enjoy your time with the people, places, and things that make your life worth living.

Close this book. Set it aside. Go now.

While your thoughts are fresh, I want you to record them. Write them down, describing them in detail.

Now, I want you to read what you have written to someone.

For most of us there are moments when we tend to make living in the material world very difficult. There are moments when we would rather be any place but where we are. Or with anybody other than whom we are with. If you doubt this, get into a car with a family of five who are vacationing away from home. You will quickly be reminded that individuals wants are often widely divergent.

Sometimes I experience this with our son Hezekiah. He's four and some of his biggest turmoils arise when mom gets a notion to clean his room. What to me is organizing and making his living space safe, to him is a mommy Tyrannosaurus turning his world upside down and displacing everything he treasures in life. My husband helped me see Hezekiah's point of view, after all there aren't too many areas of control in a four-year-old's life. Once I expanded my consciousness, common ground and interconnectedness reigned in our household again. Now I clean as part of our time together, sometimes Kie helps, sometimes he doesn't. But he's there to let me know if I'm treading on territory best left undisturbed.

How we view life is separate from our ability to create it. Those who have learned this secret recognize difficulties always pass. They know that "ten fools can make a Hades out of Heaven, and one wise man a Heaven out of Hell." The will to choose empowers us to create a heaven or a hell out of our time on earth.

When people come together to accomplish a common goal, magic occurs. Whether a vacationing family, the people of a company, or citizens of a nation, the connecting of hearts and minds is the strength of any union and what makes our highest ideals achievable.

People come together for many reasons. Students and teachers meet on the fields of learning. Buyers and sellers meet in the marketplaces. A male and a female are drawn to one another because of compatible needs for completeness.

Sometimes an inner spiritual need connects us with others. This is the place religion has held in every civilization on earth. Spiritual communion with others connects us in thought. Spiritual communion, or worship, is a time when we can focus our minds and hearts toward the highest, greatest, best, within ourselves. Spiritual communion is essential to our well-being as a community of people. It enables us to know one another as brothers and sisters and gives us reason to pause in our interactions with one another.

In church or at temple or at synagogue, spiritual communion gives us time to evaluate how we worship God, what our relationship with God is, who God is, and why that God exists.

Then we come away and our life looks differently to us. At least for a while nothing is the same. Everything is changed because our awareness is changed. Spiritual renewal is an excellent reason to go to church regularly, spiritual progression is another.

It is my hope that the exercise at the opening of this chapter afforded you a moment of spiritual communion, first with yourself, and then with the person with whom you shared your thoughts. Perhaps you wrote about one of the following. These areas of endeavor are universals that may have crossed your mind in thinking about what is most important to you.

You may have said that education is important to you or your schooling. Maybe traveling is important, or new things. Perhaps you described your job or career as being particularly valuable to you.

You may have said your relationships are the most important to you. A spouse. A friend, a loved one. That love is important to you. That having someone to lean on every once in a while is important. Having someone to talk to who will listen, or being able to listen to someone else. Or just having someone to share with, someone to be with, is valuable.

For those with children, they are cited as an important and integral part of life.

Some hold expressions of self such as artwork as an essential part of life. Or the ability to construct with wood and nails. For such a one creating change, taking something and modeling it into something different, is important.

Some say position is important. Being able to lead people, having something of value to say that you know will aid someone else, is important. This person values teaching and its progenitor, wisdom.

The world is a vast place. A vast schoolroom offering many classes. Every time I think about this my mind immediately goes to the fact that, for those interested in spiritual discipline as you and I are, we have lived many, many lifetimes. By now we have experienced six, maybe even seven continents, over hundreds of time periods, with countless numbers of souls. We have studied in Greece with Socrates or lived a monastic life in China or been a slave in Egypt or fished in the fjords of Norway. There aren't too many of those classes that we haven't taken at least once and some many times.

There just aren't too many physical experiences that we haven't had.

The purpose of our physical existence and knowing what is important to us must eventually come to a point of evolution, of realizing that each one of us truly is a channel for the Lord. Whether you think that Lord is outside of you or you perceive the Lord as inside of you, ultimately makes no difference. The choices we make in our experiences in life are a way that we can manifest, that we can bring into being, that we can share and know what the Lord is.

What is important to you is important to other people.

Sometimes I think we put ourselves down, thinking what we have to say is not important, or what we have to offer is not important. That is never true.

It can be a convenient excuse for us not to do something for a while.

The world would be different if you were not here.

One who reasons at some time asks, "How will the world be different *because* I am here?"

In this light "importance" begins to take on a different dimension and Spiritual Renaissance has dawned in the mind of one more person.

There is a wonderful story from the *Upanishads*. It illustrates very well the factors of importance. It is a very visual story, so use your mental eye to conjure the images the words describe.

Long ago a great monster enclosed all the waters of the earth. There was a terrible drought and famine swept the world. Indra was a god who walked on the earth, and so it took him quite a while to realize he had the power to free the world. Indra had a box of thunderbolts. All he had to do to free the world was strike the monster dead. When he did, the waters flowed and the world was refreshed.

Pleased with himself, Indra said, "What a good boy am I!"

Impressed by his ingenuity, Indra goes up to the cosmic mountain, the central mountain of the world, and decides to build a palace worthy of one such as he.

The main carpenter of the gods toils incessantly to please the god. Each time Indra comes to inspect the progress, he has bigger ideas about how splendid and grandiose the palace should be. Finally the carpenter realizes, "There is no end to his desires! We are both immortal, I am caught for eternity!" Panicked he goes to Brahma, the creator God, to seek help.

Brahma sits on a lotus, the symbol of divine energy and divine grace. The lotus grows from the navel of Vishnu who is the sleeping God whose dream is the universe. The carpenter comes to the edge of the great lotus pond of the universe and tells his story to Brahma. Brahma says, "Go home. I will take care of this."

Brahma descends his lotus and kneels down to address sleeping Vishnu. Vishnu gestures slightly, as if to say, "It is acknowledged."

The next morning at the gate of the growing palace a beautiful blue-black boy appears. Seated on his throne Indra, the king God, says, "Young man welcome. What brings you to my palace?"

The boy, voice like thunder rolling on the heavens, says, "I have been told that you are building such a palace as no Indra before has ever built."

"Indras before me, young man? What are you talking about?"

The boy replies, "Indras before you. I have seen them come. I have seen them go. Come and go. Vishnu sleeps in the cosmic ocean, the lotus of the universe growing from his navel. On the lotus sits Brahma, the Creator. Brahma opens his eyes and a world comes into being, governed by an Indra. Brahma closes his eyes and a world goes out of being. The life of a Brahma is 432,000 years. When he dies the lotus goes back and another lotus is formed, and another Brahma.

"Think of the galaxies, and even beyond, in infinite spaces. Each a lotus, with a Brahma sitting on it, opening his eyes, closing his eyes.

"And Indras! There may be wise men in your court who would volunteer to count the drops of water in the oceans of the world or the grains of sand on the beaches but no one would count those Brahma, let alone those Indras."

While the boy is talking, an army of ants parades across the floor. The boy laughs when he sees them, and Indra's hair stands on end and he says to the boy, "Why do you laugh?"

The boy answers, "Don't ask unless you are willing to be hurt."

Indra says, "I ask. Teach."

The boy points to the ants and says, "Former Indras all. Through many lifetimes they rise from the lowest conditions to the highest illumination and then they drop their thunderbolt on a monster and they say, 'What a good boy am I!' And down they go again."

While the boy is talking a crotchety old yogi comes into the palace with a banana leaf parasol. He is naked except for a loin cloth. On his chest is a little wisp of hair and half the hairs in the middle have all dropped out. The boy greets him and asks him just what the Indra was about to ask, "Old man what is your name? Where do you come from? Where is your family? Where is your house? And what is the meaning of this curious constellation of hair on your chest!?"

"Well," says the old fellow, "My name is hairy. I don't have a house, life is too short for that. I just have this parasol. I don't have a family, I just meditate on Vishnu's feet and think of eternity, and how time is passing. You know every time an Indra dies a world disappears. Every time an Indra dies one hair drops out of this circle on my chest. Half of the hairs are gone now. Pretty soon they will all be gone. Life is short. Why build a house?"

Then the two disappeared. The boy was Vishnu, the Lord Protector, and the old Yogi was Shiva, the creator and destroyer of the world, who had just come for the instruction of Indra who is simply a god of history but believes he is the entire memory.

Seated on his throne, Indra is completely disillusioned. Completely empty. He calls the carpenter and says, "I'm not going to build this palace, you can go."

His desire fulfilled, he says, "Hallelujah." He is dismissed from the job and there is no more construction.

Indra decides to become a yogi and just meditate on the lotus feet of Vishnu. But he has a beautiful queen named Indrani. When Indrani hears of Indra's plans she goes to the gods and says, "Now he has the idea that he can be a yogi."

"Well," says the priest, "come in and sup with me and we'll work this all out."

They sit before the king's throne and the priest says, "Now I wrote a book for you many years ago on the art of politics. You were in the position of the king of the Gods, you are a manifestation of the mystery of Brahma in the field of time. This is a high privilege. Appreciate it. Honor it and deal with life as though you were what you really are. I am going to write you a book on the art of love so you and your wife will know that in the wonderful mystery of the two that are one the Brahma is radiantly present also."

With these instructions, Indra gives up his idea of becoming a yogi and finds that in life he can represent the eternal as a symbol of the Brahma.

Indra is everyone. Everyone who is discovering there is more to life than they had suspected. Everyone who yearns to do well and be recognized or accepted for it. Everyone who wants to make a difference in the world.

Indra is the one who learns from his experiences. The one who comes to know there is more to existence than what the material world can contemplate. The one who replaces his lust for personal success with a desire for spiritual union. Indra is the one who recognizes the illusion and the meaning of our physical lives.

The material world is our schoolroom. There are many classes offered, by many teachers at many times. Although we are not all taking the same classes, I believe we are all pursuing the same degree. That degree has been described in every Holy scripture passed down from generation to generation. For now, let's call it a degree in Self Mastery.

Life is filled with moments that we turn into hours or days or years or lifetimes. What we share in common with the great people of history, those renaissance men and women, is time. What distinguishes us is how we use the time we have. That is a result of the quality of our thoughts, how we think, more than what we think. How we use the choices that we make determines the scope and meaning of our lives.

Eventually, like Indra, we come to know that meaning of life is even beyond the yogic awareness, the Christ awareness, the Cosmic awareness. Meaning pours forth from being, from *represent(ing) the eternal as a symbol of the Brahma.* Surrendering ourselves to the higher good makes us a channel for the Supreme Power in everything that we do, everything that we say, every action we make. We are undergoing a renaissance of spirit. Our lives are forever changed.

The story of Indra illustrates well one of the laws that govern creation, the Law of Relativity. By applying in life what I learn and teaching what works to others, I have come to understand the Law of Relativity as it applies to individual thinking. As you give, so you receive. One thing leads to another. As above, so below. There is cause and effect in our lives, particularly in relationship to the material and ethereal worlds. Our night time dreams are relative to our everyday waking existence. Intuition is relative to reasoning, memory relative to imagination.

Relativity reaches its fruition through husband and wife, parent and child, brother and sister. Familial relations provide a place for each of us, as symbolized in Indra and Indrani, to experience the love of the Creator (Brahma). Just as two are one, so a hundred thousand or a billion are one when the Source of the love is present. This calls upon another law of the universe, the Law of Infinity. When the laws are coordinated the experience is no longer linear. "One thing leads to another" no longer describes only a physical progression, like dominos falling down or good networking of one person talking to another to another so that the first person obtains something desired. Now "one thing leads to another" transcends the material world becoming a process of illumination that includes the whole self. Now we are living the *process*, the movement of one thing that is leading to another and another, rather than attached to what the things are. We reap understanding from our experience. Like Indra we are wielding our godlike powers. We are becoming creators.

A question has often occurred to me that I want to pass on to you because every time I think about it, it serves me well and perhaps it will you also. I have often wondered *how many understandings an individual can gain from a single experience.*

I have often used this idea as a test for myself in making sure that I make the most of every moment. That I learn the most I can. That I give what learning and wisdom I have to the best of my ability.

If we are to utilize the Law of Relativity with the Law of Infinity then there is another question we ask, *"How many understandings are possible by many individuals who experience the same physical condition?"* This is the epitome of interconnectedness. We've all experienced some type of class during our lives. Whether marriage or children or commerce, the stimulus for learning is neutral, our response to the stimulus individual. How many understandings did we gain? The number is truly infinite. Think about common experiences, the first landing of a man on the moon and the assassination of President John F. Kennedy stand out in my mind. I was young and these events left a lifelong impression on my consciousness. I used to believe it was the emotional impact that the memory endured, and undoubtedly emotion is there. Now I realize it was the sustained interconnectedeness with others that left the deepest, and most meaningful, impression. It strengthened my personal recognition of community with my countrymen, and in large part with the world.

For years this unconsciously operated within me, like Indra in his early phase when he has yet to learn that many Indras have come and gone. Consciousness did not lessen my sense of self importance, rather it put it in perspective. I was ready to tackle whether a falling tree makes a sound when there is no one there to hear it, or how an American hummingbird's wings influences the weather in Sydney. From a papal visit to a Super Bowl, the interconnectedness is apparent even when we lack knowledge of the forces of consciousness at work. Spiritual Renaissance demands such knowledge and the wisdom it can draw forth.

When we become aware of the movement of these two laws in our consciousness, we begin to open the number of inner channels for giving and receiving. We can sense the vibratory pattern of creation and respond to it. Our capacity to interpret energies is enhanced. Describe the difference between the consciousness in Los Angeles and Cairo. The Alamo and Stonehenge. A rock concert and the singing of Handel's "Messiah." The Olympics and a family picnic in the park. In each case people make the difference because we are the ones who cause something to be what it is. We only realize the difference by giving our thought completely to something.

Undivided attention is the skill that enables you to focus upon a single point. As you master attention it gives you the ability to perceive 360°. The resulting expansion of consciousness reveals the interconnectedness of all. You give completely, you receive in like kind.

When we include all people of any race, any religion, any

country, any educational background in our thinking, we begin to understand our own importance individually. We appreciate our relation with others. We love completely, free of attachments born from egocentric needs. We learn to be in the world but not of it.

We now have an expanded awareness of the lessons in life. They are more than lessons of physical endurance or memorizing parts of speech. They are more than choices that will pass the time we call life. Expand your awareness beyond the material realm. When education, career, newness, learning, are important to you realize these are more than something to do. They are expressions of your inner urge for learning. Become sensitive to this inner urge and actively respond to it! It has been said talent does what it can, genius does what it must. Get in contact with your genius, discover what it is you *must* do. Be willing to do whatever may be required.

When your spouse, friends, relationships are important to you, realize these reflect your inner urge for wholeness, completeness, partnership, cooperation. Practice the eleventh commandment given by Jesus, "Love ye one another." Endeavor to love completely, without restriction or expectation of having your love returned.

When your children are important to you realize this symbolizes your inner urge to create in your likeness and in your image. Our offspring stimulate awareness of the continuity of being and the delight in creation. Allow their youthful innocence to fill you, opening your mind to seeing life from fresh perspectives. Interacting with children frees you from the heavy chains of prejudice and bigotry. Giving them your best counsel brings forth the spiritual teacher in you.

When communication is important to you. Realize this is our inner urge for compatibility. The capacity to speak a common language is essential for others to understand you and for you to understand them. The common language all of mankind speaks is images, the language used in the inner levels of consciousness, the language of your dreams. Learn to think in images. Draw on your experience before speaking. Describe your experiences with your words. In this way you will begin aligning the outer mind with the inner mind and communicating your ideas will come easier; so will listening to receive other's ideas. Still your mind in order to receive someone else's thoughts as well as their words. Daily, you will realize the truth, "Do unto others as you would have them do unto you."

These are lessons which bring awareness of God into our experience.

When we bring God into our experience we contact the universal. When we bring God into our experience our innate desire for spirituality is fulfilled. Our spirit is transformed.

Years ago I had an opportunity to ask a wise spiritual teacher a question. My question was, "What is most important to you?"

The reason I asked that question I wanted to know from her perspective what was most important. I wanted to hear her thoughts because her realm of experience was so different from mine. The depth of her intuitive insight was so keen, I wanted to see the world through her eyes.

You know what her response was? She didn't tell me that learning was the most important thing. She didn't tell me that wisdom was the most important. Or love. Or beauty. Or having a job. Or getting up on time. Or having children.

When I asked, "What is most important to you?" The teacher replied, "What is most important to you?"

And I answered her. The first thing I said was "love." The second thing I said was "wisdom." The third thing I said was "growth."

She said, "Yes, all those things are important. But don't fail to make Barbara important." That took me aback. For someone who had been raised to humble herself, to be thankful for her good fortune and never be too full of herself, this brought both courage and fear. Then she referred back to something we had spoken of earlier, she said, "That's why there is that place inside that isn't filled up. And you'll have to make Barbara important to fill it."

People have taught me that this counsel is much more than personally revelatory, it is universally applicable. I know that our activities in the material world can be very empty. I know that we can wonder why we even bother to get up in the morning. Or why we are staying at a job, or in a dissatisfying relationship. Or why we should even have to open our mouths and say anything. Why can't people just read our minds?

Every why opens a door. Each door leads to heaven or it leads to hell. You choose.

Our need is for inner awareness. When we live our lives heedlessly, our activities seem empty and of little importance.

When we live our lives mindfully we open ourselves to illumination. Like Indra we give up our idea of becoming a yogi or a doctor or a parent or an executive because we realize these are only the opportunities for awareness. For one who thinks of the physical aspects of life only, roles in life are the goal, the end. For one who thinks spiritually, the roles become the means to bring enlightenment. In this way we find that in life we, too, can represent the eternal as a symbol of the Brahma.

Individually, and collectively as a society, we must learn from our own experiences while developing the necessary mental skills to gain understanding from "walking in another's shoes." Reasoning produces the former; intuition the latter.

A Love for Truth

an essay first published in August 1997

Prom night. How can parents make sure their kids live through it without killing themselves and each other? Find out.....

Older citizens. What happens when we live past the age we've financially prepared for?

Child care. Is your child receiving the kind of attention you are paying for?

If the current media is to be believed, people only learn from fear.

Turn on any newscast. Within the first five minutes what do you hear? Reports of man's goodness? His generosity to his fellow man? His wisdom, honor, and integrity? Stories that inspire us of people we want to emulate?

What is reported as news and how it is reported purports to represent us as a people. Over the years I have met thousands of people from all points on the globe, corresponded with as many, and through electronic media enjoyed conversations with millions. A relatively large representation of humanity that leads me to a very different image of mankind than the one flickering on the evening news. In spite of the racy, "push it to the limit", "appeal to their baser instinct" reporting, mankind is rapidly outgrowing the limits of media's recording of history.

There are many who are evolving into a spiritual adulthood characterized by a genuine willingness to provide a higher quality of life for everyone on the planet.

Hard work reveals genius, and genius gives the world beauty it has never before known.

When you meet people face-to-face, when you talk with them one-on-one, you discover the truth.

Beyond the magnetic tape is a far more attractive reality. Beyond the pieces of sentences, soundbites they are called, purposefully-chosen to be aired, are the paragraphs that tell the whole story. It is the whole story which leads to the truth, to tell less distorts the truth, filtering it through someone else's bias. The sin of omission, whether between a husband and wife or between those who own public media and those who trust it, is a cancer that erodes our belief in ourselves, retarding the potential and eventually destroying the good. Truth must be valued more highly in our individual consciousness and in our collective consciousness.

Fear arises from what is unknown. It is the result of an undisciplined imagination. "But," you say, "what about the child who is molested by a relative, or the person who drives on icy roads and wrecks his car? These fears aren't imagined; they actually happened. These are known occurrences." Yes, this is true. If they do happen to you it becomes a part of your experience, a fact of your life. Will the child tell someone about the relative or hide it, thus inadvertently opening the door for it to happen again and feeding fears? Will the driver admit his impatience because he was late or his distraction because he was talking on a car phone instead of driving or his negligence in car maintenance? When the experience is yours so are the choices. The truth is what we *do* with the facts, *how we think about them*, determines the reality. The truth does set us free. Free from ignorance. Free from danger.

Free from fear.

As a society we do not as yet know how to learn through observation. When we receive reports of crises happening to someone somewhere else in the world, we do not have the direct experience to draw upon, so we are at a loss to identify why it may have occurred. We can only imagine: how horrible it must have been, how painful for the families, it could have been my neighbor, could it happen to me?

Daily we are bombarded with words and pictures of human tragedy that provoke our imaginations. Any balance point that teaches us self control and self determination is sorely lacking in mass communication. We are left to our own initiative. Some people are moved to action that will seek an end to the suffering they witness. Most shy away from what they see, ignoring it, pretending the images only exist on celluloid, or they find themselves consumed by the tragedies, protecting themselves from imagined harm.

Individually, and collectively as a society, we must learn from our own experiences while developing the necessary mental skills to gain understanding from "walking in another's shoes." Reasoning produces the former; intuition the latter. Reasoning frees us to productively use memory and imagination to expand the scope of our experience while giving that experience depth and meaning. As we cultivate intuition, drawing upon our souls' storehouse of understanding, we can expect to grasp Truth through expanded awareness as well as direct experience. Living the truth is the place to begin.

World-renowned talk show host, Oprah Winfrey, organized people to tell the truth for just one day, all day.

It proved to be a remarkable challenge to some, but almost all found it was easy to tell the truth about the "big things" and more difficult with the small things. People became caught up in what they imagined others would think instead of exploring their own thoughts. *"This above all,"* wrote Shakespeare, *"To thine own Self be true, and it must follow as night the day that thou canst be false to any man."* When we can move our sense of what is important from imagined fears of other's judgements to a love for the Truth we will find ourselves wiser, stronger, and freer.

As we strive for Truth within ourselves, we will become less fascinated with weakness and our society will change. The way media sells itself will reflect those changes. Eventually we will leave behind media that entertains Human Man and we will begin using mass communication as a means for educating Spiritual man. That is a world well worth envisioning.

When we make Truth important in our lives we transform the way we see ourselves and each other. Our consciousness is elevated and our spirit renewed. We are free to hope, to dream, to believe, to aspire. That is our true nature, and it is where we learn best.

VIII

The Spiritual Renaissance Quest

"The great man
is he who does not lose his child's heart."

– Mencius, Chinese Sage (335-289 BC)

"Going back to the origin is called peace;
it means reversion to destiny.
Reversion to destiny is called eternity.
He who knows eternity is called enlightened."

– Lao-tzu, Chinese philosopher c. 500 BC

Spiritual Quest
Meeting God Face to Face

Based upon a talk entitlted "The Courage to Talk with God" delivered during the 12th General Assembly of the Interfaith Church of Metaphysics , January 1989..

Take a moment to imagine.

I want you to imagine, to visualize in your mind's eye, the room you are in. Begin to fill the room with people.

It probably won't take long for the people to spill out of the room into the hall, throughout the house or building and into the streets of the community. That's okay. Keep filling the room with people.

Maybe you know the people. Maybe they are people you have seen in movies or books or people who exist in your imagination. Perhaps they are people that you want to meet someday.

Fill the room with all of the people in the world. It will go beyond your city, your country but that is as is should be.

Imagine all the people in the world standing shoulder to shoulder. Can you see it?

Every one of these individuals is seeking. They look for a lot of things but each one is seeking a common something. This is why we call all people humanity. We are a part of that swell of sentient beings who have the capacity to think and to reason. We possess the great challenge of the gift of understanding.

This something that man is seeking has been described in different ways throughout his time of searching. "It" has been called the wind. "It" has been called the rain.

The something, the "It", is known as Ahura Mazda.

"It" is known as Krishna.

"It" is known as Allah.

The Hebrew and the Jew call "It" God.

In the early days of Reasoning Man – the collective consciousness comprised of memory, volition, and imagination – the Neanderthal and Cro-Magnon periods of physical history also known as the Atlantean periods in metaphysical history, man sought to understand himself in relationship to that which he did not understand. He began to wield hand tools. This was the beginning of respecting power. The power he called by different names. For now we will use the name God to describe the Source or Supreme Origin of this power.

During this time God was the sun, the physical sun. The Egyptians gave the power of the sun the name Ra. Man was dependent upon Ra for light, for gathering food or hunting prey or being protected from predators. He was dependent upon "It" for light in order to use the senses and survive. He was dependent upon "It" sometimes for warmth. He was dependent upon "It" for his own physical existence, therefore it held great power in his life.

Until he made fire! When man was able to make fire, he had a light that he learned how to carry. As a creator, he was no longer dependent upon the sun. He could make his own light. He could make his own heat. So man stopped worshiping the sun and began to worship the elements. He began to think that's god. The "It" is in the elements.

The wind is god.

The water is god.

The earth is god.

Fire is god.

We were dependent upon these for our existence until we again evolved, this time realizing we could control fire. We could produce it and handle it. We could harness water, we could channel it to meet our needs. It was no longer more powerful than us. We could even harness the wind to our advantage. The earth that was barren, we could make fertile. We were understanding how to use the elements to our advantage and with that understanding "It" moved from what was now known to the unknown once again.

We began to look for some other way we could know god. We looked toward animals. Animals had a certain kind of power that man feared as well as respected. They often threatened man's life. They seemed to hold the power of life and death, and for this reason many religious customs forbade killing animals or eating their flesh.

Again, we were dependent upon something outside ourselves. Animals provided us with food and clothing. There were certain conditions where animals were very useful and we began to study and learn about their instincts and habits. Evidence of the idea of worshipping animals exists in cave drawings, in carvings and statues around the world. The more we understand the differences between man and animals the more distance we cause and "It" again evolves as we ourselves do. Becoming knowledgeable is one of the advantages of science for it adds to our understanding of the Universe. "It" now embodies supernatural powers, instantaneous healing, elimination of evil and exaltation of good, restoration of spirit. "It" is the oracle of all unknown.

In these ways we have evolved in our thinking about God.

Most people of the Earth worship in some form a Maker or progenitor of the Universe.

We know god in places. Christians place God in heaven, which separates him from us. Some place God in things. Some make money their god. Others make a desired position in society their god. Others, a possession. Think of people who won't go anywhere without their crystal or rosary.

Then there are people who put god in people. Think of religious leaders. It doesn't matter if you agree with their philosophies. From the Catholic Pope to Martin Luther King to Mohandas K. Gandhi such leaders are charismatic, and many equate the message with the messenger. They confuse the Maker with what has been made. Then there are those who find it quite fashionable to put god inside themselves, to say "I'm a god."

The reality is that God is everywhere. Omnipresent. The American Sioux Indian tell stories of the Great Spirit, Wakantaka.

In hopes of learning the great wisdom, a youth studied the mysteries under a medicine man who told him, "This world is comprised of four colors: red for the sun, blue for the sky, green for the earth, and yellow for the rock. Go, find the great rock where the colors meet."

The youth journeyed, uncertain of his destination but very sure of his reason and right in the journey. He was gone for many years.

Upon returning, the medicine man embraced him, asking what he had seen. The youth replied, "As the colors are united in the rainbow, so are all things united in Wakantaka."

The medicine man was pleased knowing that such an answer would only come from one ready to be tested. The training began as the elder asked, "Who is the oldest?"

"Rock is the oldest, the grandfather," the youth replied.

"Who is the next oldest?" "Earth is the next oldest, the grandmother."

"Who is the next oldest?" "Sky is the next oldest, giver of life and motion."

"Who is the next oldest? Sun is the next oldest, above us."

With this the medicine man knew the youth had seen the

elk. He bestowed his blessing upon him and accepted the youth into his abode.

The Sioux believe the first elk appeared on top of the primeval rock and bayed loudly. In answer, the first dawn rose out of the dark abyss which confronted the rock. The elk, the rock, the dawn, and the abyss are all Wakantaka and this is the great wisdom known by the many and practiced by only the chosen few.

For centuries mankind has believed understanding the Creator is necessary for his survival. The sense that knowing his Origin will help him to understand his own existence and the purpose for his existence has been present in mankind throughout the ages. The truth of this sense has prevailed, time and time again. Every great civilization that incorporates spirituality into the fiber of its being flourishes. When spirituality is absent or wanes, the civilization crumbles.

Miraculous advances have occurred since the European Renaissance, from industry to technology, from living in isolation to windows on the world, from the necessity of a mediator between man and God to internalization of deity. It is a recent development that we are beginning to personalize our relationship with our Maker. No longer do we believe we are unworthy, whether in station or condition of birth, or in the character. We no longer require an intermediary, thus we no longer separate ourselves from our origin and our destiny. Increasing numbers of people are nurturing a relationship with their Maker in hopes of coming to know the mind of God. This commitment births new awareness, an expansion of consciousness that opens the mind to God. We come to know that God is everywhere, in every experience. God is creation.

The quest of the metaphysician is to know God exists *from personal experience.* Daily we experience God with the inner senses as well as the outer ones. We leave behind the question of God's existence. Our scientific approach to religious philosophy demands experimentation and results. A metaphysician uses the five physical senses purposefully by employing the sense of the mind, mental attention. The mind interprets what the body is seeing, hearing, smelling, tasting, and feeling. You can move beyond the compulsions of letting the body do as it will. Having built a strong will-power opens your consciousness to recognizing "It's" power on a new and deeper level.

We do not have to be told of God's existence, we *know* that God exists. We can describe "It". We can tell others what God looks like, and feels like, and sounds like. With developed mental perception God can be perceived everywhere, and in everything. God is creation. Everywhere you look, everything you see, everything you hear, everything you smell and taste and feel is God.

The *Bhagavad Gita* is a story about a prince who wrestles with his own understanding of God and how he can become more perfect, more God-filled, God-like. The beauty of Prince Arjuna's story is that he learns, he progresses, he evolves his understanding.

Arjuna is one of five Pandu princes. The five Pandu princes represent our five physical senses. Arjuna symbolizes the conscious, waking mind of the person who is developing the use of sight. Such a person is learning to see the world around him with in-sight.

Arjuna makes changes throughout the discourse in the *Gita*. The changes occur because he is communicating with a character named Krishna. Symbolically, Krishna represents the I Am, the individual expression of God within each of us. The story is parallel in symbolic meaning to the last book of the *Bible*, the *Revelation of John*. However the action in the *Gita* is described somewhat differently than in the Bible. Both books are written in a wholistic language, the Universal Language of Mind. The *Revelation* is filled with images, shocking to the conscious mind, nonexistent in our physical world and to some unimaginable. Yet when interpreted in the Universal Language the meaning is the same as the images revealed in the social intercourse in which the *Gita* is penned.

There is a great beauty in studying the *Gita* following familiarity with the *Bible* which is how it came into my life. In the *Gita*, Arjuna will talk for a while and then Krishna will talk for a while. They listen to one another. Not since the early days recorded in the *Old Testament* – the talks between Abraham and the Lord, David and the Lord, or Solomon and the Lord – has man enjoyed such extensive divine intercourse. Arjuna brings this inner discourse into our present stage of evolution as full-fledged beings, reasoners seeking spiritual unfoldment.

Through the communion between the outer, conscious mind (Arjuna) and the innermost divine Self (Krishna), humanity learns how to evolve beyond using solely the outer senses to experience. Now we can directly grasp the truth by drawing upon mental perception – the sixth sense. This so aptly describes where mankind stands today. We are at this wonderful stage of development. We are able to take advantage of everything we worked so hard to make second nature. Now we can embrace this innate sense of truth and refine it into a spiritual reality.

When I was young, my parents and grandparents taught me that God was everywhere. They taught me I could talk with Him, in fact God was the last person I talked with every night. It would be years before I would realize the breadth of what I was making a part of my consciousness in these nightly talks with my Maker.

We would go to church several times a week. People in our church were hearty prayers. They were strictly disciplined in their everyday life and so they saved their "joyful noises" for Sunday morning. I remember one Sunday, listening to all these people praying. Out loud. At the same time. I was amazed. Until that time I had imagined that God had two ears, just like me. After all I had been taught I was made in his likeness! But suddenly it occurred to me, "God must have ears everywhere!" I believed, and I knew, that God heard prayers. I had learned from going to school that there were a lot of churches and a lot of people meeting at the same time, especially on Sunday, and if they were all praying He would have to have even more ears than I could ever imagine.

As I neared adolescence I started experiencing things I didn't understand. It seemed God didn't always answer the prayers of people. It didn't seem to be the ones who prayed the loudest, or the longest, or the most beautifully, whom God heard.

I reached a point of disillusion. I noticed that often prayers of truly good people, people I knew deserved better, weren't always answered, and I didn't understand that. It did not fit with my idea of God I felt so sure inside that God was just and loving and true. But the physical evidence was confusing. I began to think you must need to be outstanding in order for God to hear you, for your request to be fulfilled. I didn't know what that outstanding feature was, and I gave up trying to figure it out for some time.

Years later after I graduated from college, I discovered the answer when I learned how to meditate. The form of meditation I learned is Superconscious Meditation taught at the School of Metaphysics. This is meditation that ultimately aligns the inner levels of consciousness for illumination, and begins with cultivating a relaxed body, calm emotions, and a still mind. With the first lesson I discovered the "something" that makes an individual outstanding enough to communicate with God and have their prayers answered. That "something" is the *ability to listen for God's response*! The outstanding feature is not our ability to talk. Nor is it our ability to physically hear. It is our ability to inwardly listen, with the mind.

To listen with the spirit. The capacity to still our mind so it can be attuned to the mind of God.

This is what occurs in the *Gita*. Arjuna learns the value of stilling his mind, and when he does a flood of guidance is presented in the form of images. All the senses are directed toward awareness of I AM, the divine spiritual essence of Self. This learning produces the ability to communicate within the seven inner levels of consciousness.

When I first studied the *Gita*, I began to change my old ideas of fearing God into new concepts of respecting God. As an adult young woman, supporting herself and living on her own, I didn't know what I was so scared about. After all my image of God was a loving one. But the old memories of reading about a wrath-filled, jealous God in the *Old Testament* in the *Bible* had left many imagined fears that it was time for me to face. I began to realize it was time to stop running from my early training, to stop denying its influence upon me, and begin to face my own thoughts.

If I was going to hold the belief that I was an offspring of God, that I have a Spiritual Parent somewhere, and I was made in the likeness and image of that Spiritual God, then I had to first let go of *thinking for* that God. I had to begin by disciplining my thoughts, so I could be open to receive who He is. That meant giving up some of those ideas. After some soul searching I vowed to cease creating God in *my* image and after *my* likeness, or the likeness of someone else in my life. It was a reasonable conclusion. People could be wrathful and jealous and even murderous. Did I believe that was God? No. Did I believe that God made people be that way? No. So how and why did "It" all come about? That question I will be answering the rest of my life.

The difference was I was no longer running from the question or the answers. I possessed a new willingness to respect, to revisit, to reconsider, to reorganize my thinking as new insights would come during meditation. I began to form an image of my worthiness as a child of God that was quickly maturing toward compatibility. I found it takes courage to talk with God, and it takes courage to listen.

I found the more I prayed and meditated, the more I understand the Holy work I am most familiar with – the *Bible*. I learned the more that I communicate, the more I meditate, the more I understand about how the whole mind functions, the more I understand the *Bible* as a remarkable textbook for the evolution of spiritual consciousness. It tells us this through a series of myths, a lineage of males that begin with God and culminate in the man Jesus who becomes known as the Christ, the son of God. The *Bible* is a book about each individual from their creation as light to their development as Spiritual Man. By linking one generation to the next to the next, major developments in the maturing of consciousness are exemplified in symbolic form.

Those who are part of the lineage that produces Spiritual Man as symbolized by Jesus communicated directly with God or the Lord God just as Arjuna does in the *Gita*. Each had the ability to communicate with the Lord. Each was a man of courage. Each played a significant part in the development of the thinker that leads to Spiritual Man. They not only spoke to God but they listened. And they acted on what they heard. You know what? Every time they did that, things worked out.

I decided it was time to emulate these men of old, and more importantly to understand more fully what they could teach me, what they might reveal to me about the three most significant questions I had ever asked.– "Where did I come from? Why am I here? Where am I going?" I found one of the greatest texts for answering these questions was that little black book that was almost as old as I.

I began studying the *Bible* in a new way. Instead of reading it, letting it sink in, praying and meditating about a passage, and responding the best I could to what I believed it was saying, I began taking a more scientific approach. I had been learning a new language, the Universal Language of Mind. This language was a picture language, the one the inner mind uses to convey its message to the outer mind in the form of dreams. I began using this language to interpret Holy scriptures, with amazing results. The Universal language of Mind was opening my eyes to Universal Truths I had been seeking for years.

By interpreting the universal images appearing in the text, I realized the wholistic nature of the teaching. Anyone reading the *Bible* in the Universal Language would derive the same truths, the same guidance, and the same instructions. Throughout the generations of the *Bible* the ideal remains the same, to reach the seventh day of creation. Every generation holds that goal holy. The commitment between the outer, conscious mind and the inner, I AM remains strong, and each successive generation adds to the awareness of who I AM until the title Christ is earned. This is a commitment that is very strong in the mind, so strong it produces an adding on with each successive individual.

There are no compromises. Abraham is the one that makes the original covenant with the Lord God. He is the "*father of a host of nations*." Then he dies without it ever happening but that's okay because his son Isaac takes over, right? No, it doesn't work that way. When you interpret the *Bible* in the Universal Language of Mind it makes sense, reasonable sense. It reveals where we come from, why we are here, where we are going. As we develop the courage to talk with God and to listen to what God has to communicate to us, we claim our birthright and receive the blessing of our heavenly Father. One of the early passages in the *Bible* teaches this concept.

There is a man in the Bible, the younger of twins, who

was destined from birth to be a "strong nation." He grew into a "plain man" who dwelled in tents, while his brother was a cunning hunter, a man of the field.

The younger was pretty sharp. He knew that he was not the firstborn. At that time and place, firstborn sons were entitled to certain things that were to be very much desired, and the second son wanted those things. One day he cooked a porridge and he waited for his brother to come home. He knew his brother would be famished from trapping, hunting. He asked his brother if he wanted some of his porridge and his brother said, "Yes."

The younger twin in exchange claimed the father's birthright. He bought it off his brother, who gave it up for a bowl of soup.

But there was something else that he wanted that would by tradition still go to his older brother. That was the father's blessing. To this end, his mother assisted him in tricking the father into giving him his blessing. If you want the details you can read about it in the Book of Genesis The father blessed him, thinking he was the elder son.

Sounds like deceit and thievery until you realize all the characters in the story represent you.

The father sent the second son on a journey where he would meet his destiny.

During this time the man had a dream. There was a ladder set on earth with its top reaching heaven. Angels of God were ascending and descending it. The Lord stood above it, and spoke to this man.

The Lord told him that he was the Lord God of Abraham his father and the God of Isaac. Now this man's physical father was not Abraham, but the Lord God told him that he was the God of his father Abraham, and the God of Isaac. He promised the man that the land he was on was his and that his seed would be "as the dust of earth" spreading to the west, to the east, to the north and to the south.

Well, the man woke up from the dream and when he woke up from the dream he thought God must be in this place. He was scared. You know, just because you have moments of being scared it doesn't make you a coward. This man woke up from his dream and he was afraid, but he made a vow even in the midst of being scared, and the vow was to God.

He vowed that if God would feed him and clothe him and be with him that he would accept him as his God.

This man was called Jacob.

Jacob was, at this point, in a state of believing. Building believing. It reminds me of my beginning meditations, where I would receive flashes of insight and momentary inspirations that I knew were right and I would act on them. Everything would turn out all right.

Jacob didn't stop with believing. He could have stopped there but he didn't. Jacob symbolizes the acceptance into your consciousness that there is one God. This leads to the awareness earned by our aspiring Sioux medicine man: that God, the Great Spirit, is ever present, within and without, neither, either, yet both. For Jacob this is described in his struggle with the angel. It is Jacob who wrestles at daybreak with the man and wins. He asks for a blessing and receives from the man a new name –*Israel* because he *"was a prince who had power with God and with men."* The only thing that separates us from God-awareness is our own undisciplined thinking. It is often a battle to quell the dark forces within and reach the new awareness symbolized by the breaking of day. The promise to one who is so disciplined is the self-mastery (prince) that frees us to create spiritually and materially.

This place, this point in evolution, is special, unlike any other. Jacob calls that place Penuel *"for I have seen God face to face and my life has been spared."*

This marks a change in our identity. We are no longer animal man, controlled by the needs of our bodies, the dictates of our senses. We are now reasoning man, reaching to transform the way we identify ourselves, breaking free of the chains that have bound us to the material world. Our destiny to become a spiritual man is cast as we cross the threshold into the renaissance.

There is order in our universe. We are so fascinated by it that we have created an entire section of human endeavor dedicated to studying it and another realm dedicated to living in harmony with it. The first we call science, the latter we call religion.

We All Pray to the Same God

an essay first published in the Fall, 1997

She could have been from any city in the United States. New York, San Antonio, or Seattle. Perhaps any city in the world. But she hailed from Buffalo, a community of 2000 in southwestern Missouri.

What struck me so profoundly about her is her desire to be open-minded, after all as a high school teacher she is entrusted daily with the fertile, growing minds of tomorrow's leaders. Yet amid all her finer qualities and best intentions, dwells the demon that disturbs the peace of many.

While attending a U.S.-China Joint Conference on Women's Issues in Beijing a couple years ago the woman took time to be a tourist, mixing with the local people and viewing the culture firsthand. Her trip included the Temple of Heaven, a succession of temples where ancient emperors went to pray.

During that tour the woman reportedly witnessed something that makes her think Chinese and Americans may one day be able to bridge the wide gap between vastly different cultures and political systems. She was apart from the group with no interpreter in sight. A Buddhist woman, children in tow, approached her and began speaking rapidly in Chinese. The American tried to explain she did not know the language and could not understand what the woman was trying to tell her. An interpreter finally appeared to bridge the communication gap.

Through the interpreter, the woman said she was praying for world peace. She gestured toward her children implying volumes without saying any words.

The American appeared to immediately embrace the woman's sincere hope and dream, saying "if everybody would pray for peace, especially mothers, there would be peace." Then she added, "I pray to a different God, but I also pray for peace."

Upon first hearing this story most of us would probably see this American in a favorable light because we would believe, should the occasion arise, our own response might be similar. But read it again. And again. And again. Read it until you actually hear what the American said.

"I pray to a different God."

This woman could not bring herself to agree. She could not simply say, "I too pray to God for peace," and rejoice in the fact that she shared something precious in common with a stranger who lives half a world away. This Christian had to reject the Buddhist and her beliefs, even as she appeared to embrace her. "Must you betray me with a kiss?" asked the Christian master Jesus of the disciple who informed political authorities of his presence.

This woman, like devotees from faiths around the world, allows her comprehension of spiritual principles to be the basis for pushing others away. It is as though she believes not in an omniscient and omnipresent Creator that exists for all of creation, but in something else. Although she would deny it, her words reveal the doubt in her mind, the demon that torments. By insisting "I pray to a different God" she abandons monotheism, the very soul of the religion she professes. She is aware of the Christian belief that "God created man in his image and after his likeness," but she has yet to fathom it. This woman lives by a God she has created in her own imagination. A God that belongs only to her and her kind, a God she will share only under certain conditions.

However well intentioned it is this kind and quality of thinking that has justified bigotry, conflict, torture, war and death for centuries. From the current brother against brother battle between the Christians and Moslems in the former Yugoslavia to the Chinese invasion and destruction of Tibet, the seeds of enmity are planted from generation to generation. Even now after 200 years of intermarriage and community-building, neighbors in U.S. cities still build fences, still lock their doors, still don't know the names of the people who live next door. Fear fuels the seeds of hatred, and where those seeds thrive peace is hard to find.

Some blame religion for our earthly problems saying we'd be better off without it. These people believe peaceful co-existence is a myth that will never be achieved because man will not surrender his faith in a Being greater than himself, a faith described and defined by the religions of the world. These myopic thinkers would do well to consider that throughout history, the belief in a power greater than the self is at its least a deterrent from evil doing and at best the inspiration for genius. It is inherent in us to imagine, to conceive, to create with thought. As English poet Robert Browning said, "Ah, but a man's reach should exceed his grasp, or what's a heaven for?"

One thing is certain. We have free will. Even when actions are curbed by tyranny, human beings still possess the freedom to think however we choose. We can choose to believe that life is part of a divine plan and everything happens for a reason that we are here to discover. Or we can choose to believe that life is chaos and we are here to make some sense of it. In choosing one view or the other, we exercise our inherent right to think, to reason, to choose, how we will see ourselves and our world.

There is order in our universe. We are so fascinated by it that we have created an entire section of human endeavor dedicated to studying it and another realm dedicated to living in harmony with it. The first we call science, the latter we call religion. Order is a state of peaceful harmony under a constituted authority. That metaphysical authority can rest in the laws that govern our universe or in that which created the laws themselves. Universal order would seem to require both.

Unbeknownst to religious zealots, like our American Christian, and to agnostic scientists is the simple truth that what we choose to call the Creator does not change who or what It is. Whatever set this universe into motion – God, the Creator, the original source, that spark of creative intelligence – exists whether we believe in Him or not. It is equally true that what we believe makes a great deal of difference in the peace of mind we experience. Confucius said it best, "He who offends the Gods has no one to whom to pray." God is a descriptive term for the progenitor of our universe – a cosmic combination of a Celestial Father corresponding to our physical father and a Mother Nature corresponding to our physical mother.

Arguments over religion boil down to "my God is better, bigger, stronger, truer, than your God." Like children on a playground we lack the understanding experience brings to realize every child sees his parent as God - a provider, a nourisher, a protector, a sage, a disciplinarian. And that is as it should be. So we must strive for a spiritual wisdom that transcends the physical limits we create. We must admit our common spiritual heritage and realize spiritual maturity.

All the great spiritual leaders have understood this. Every sacred scripture in the world describes it. Yet on the whole this realization continues to elude humanity.

Perhaps it is because we limit our experience of God when we are swayed by the name, or the dress, or the rituals, or the place of worship, to condemn another. As if we are right, and all others are wrong. We are good, and they are evil. This us/them mentality breeds discord at its best and hatred at its worst. Here, in our own thinking, are the seeds of man's inhumanity to his own kind. This arrogance is borne from ignorance for it lacks the humility that springs from truth that does not owe its existence to the temporal world. As His Holiness the Dalai Lama insightfully remarks, "We need to clarify the distinction between compassion and attachment, and between anger and hatred. Such clarity is useful in our daily life and in our efforts toward world peace." As the motto of the Universal Hour of Peace says, "Living peaceably begins by thinking peacefully." This is the seed idea that will mature into world peace. Government and laws cannot change the mind or heal the heart, only the individual can bring such transformations. For peace to prevail on Earth, we must move our consciousness to transcend whatever separates us. As we give love and respect, dignity and comfort, we will come to know peace. The collective attachment to diversity will pale in the brilliance of what unites us as one people.

Just decades ago American minister and civil liberties activist Martin Luther King said, "I have a dream that one day on the red hills of Georgia, the sons of former slaves and the sons of former slave-owners will be able to sit together at the table of brotherhood. That my four little children will one day live in a nation where they will not be judged by the color of their skin but by the content of their character." Daily his dream is becoming reality as increasing numbers of people envision a better way to think, a better way to live. We are going beyond our physical prejudices. The challenge of the future is releasing spiritual biases. Transcending any limits in our understanding of our own faith, believing that we will be spiritually strengthened, not diminished, by embracing others, by loving our neighbor as we love ourselves. This is not a Christian tenet alone. Every Holy Scripture expresses this sentiment thereby encouraging respect, cooperation, and understanding in its devotee. A willingness to learn of other faiths, to study the world's most valued scriptures, magnifies the truth that applies to all of mankind. This is the essence of interfaith. When you hear the concept "love your neighbor as yourself" in ten different languages you are amazed by the universality of truth.

We all pray to the same God. Whether Christian, Jew, Buddhist, Muslim, Jain, Taoist. The sooner our consciousness expands to realize this Universal Truth, the sooner we can expect to be able to turn to our neighbor and see not race, age or gender but a spiritual brother or sister desiring the same communion with our Maker that we do.

Whether you call your Creator God, Jehovah, Allah, Tao, Brahma, Ahura-Mazda, does not make the difference in your character. What does make the difference is relishing the fact that you can even conceive such a Creator and aspire to know Him. The prayer you pray is more a reflection of who you are than the intelligence for whom it is intended. The reality you live is a manifestation of your way of thinking.

Living peaceably begins by thinking peacefully. As the American in China said, "If everybody would pray for peace, there would be peace." Let us fulfill that prophecy at noon GMT on January 1. Let us create a *Universal Hour of Peace,* filling our minds and hearts with peace, then go forth into a new year making peace with ourselves and our neighbors, being living examples of the metaphysical truths we learn from our religions.

We will spread peace across the face of the earth. One person at a time.

X

The Spiritual Renaissance Destiny

"The light of God surrounds me,
The love of God unfolds me,
The power of God protects me,
The Presence of God watches over me,
Wherever I am, God is."
– Christian Prayer Card

"The destiny of man is in his own soul."
– Herodotus, Greek historian (484-425 BC)

Spiritual Destiny
Revelation of God in Man

Based upon an Interfaith sermon delivered during SOM National Teachers Conference, October, 1992.

While technology has eased many of the tasks mankind believes to be burdens it makes new demands upon us. Our response-ability is less and less to the physical world and more and more to the metaphysical world.

The more technology pervades a culture, the less physical energy man is required to use. Just a century ago, and still common practice in most of the world today, each family grew their own food or hunted prey, preserved it for later consumption, prepared it before eating, and cleaned after the meal. This process devoured time. Without modern conveyances, people stay close to home, with their family and neighbors, people like them. For a technological society, the only thing left for us to do is to eat.

The greatest advantage of technology is also its greatest challenge. How do we pass the "extra" time we inherit as a result of others' genius.

It may seem a needless consideration for some, but the truth is answering this question may indeed shed light on the solutions to planetary ills; overpopulation, starvation, pollution, crime. What happens to someone with too much time on their hands? My grandmother was fond of a Biblical proverb, *"Idle hands are the devil's workshop."* And so I have repeatedly realized the wisdom in her teaching.

In reality, genius is born from interaction. A creator creates.

A creator does not live his life being waited on by others. One of the greatest of human weaknesses is insolence. One of the greatest strengths of a reasoning being is generosity.

The capacity to give, freely, completely, without thought of personal recompense describes every soul who has exhibited genius. I think about Marie Curie's death from radium poisoning. Or Michelangelo's spinal degeneration during the almost two decades painting the ceiling of the Sistine Chapel.

Genius works because it must. Theirs are inventive minds. They are tireless workers. To the unenlightened, their lives are possessed by their physical passion; the knowledgeable make time to learn more. Through a careful study of these men and women, they come to know the character of the genius. And in that, reveal to themselves ideals worthy of adopting for the Self.

This is one of the greatest gifts of technology. It makes our world a smaller place. Without modern conveyances, people stay close to home, with their family and neighbors, people with the same background, education, beliefs, attitudes. People similar to them. Technology brings people of the world into our homes. It opens the meta-physical world more commonly called cyberspace. A world where we ultimately discover we are one people, one race.

I think it is a responsibility of every metaphysician to know what is going on in the world around us. I enjoy reading. Sometimes I enjoy watching the news, sometimes it irritates me, yet it is a welcome window to the world. Television enables me to know the state of the spirit of the world.

Too often during the last decade of the 1900's, items of the kind I will cite here were considered news worthy. They illustrate a certain type of consciousness that you and I are willing to accept. In fact, that you and I, either actively or passively, are willing to promote. It is worthy of our consideration to see if that is really the consciousness that we believe, or that we live, and if it truly reflects our own ideas of spirituality.

The first was a short article appearing in the *Wall Street Journal,* a widely read New York City paper, on Wednesday, September 30, 1992. This was an election year for the United States, a year when a president would be elected. The man in office proposed several public debates that would allow the two major candidates to speak their minds and present their policies to the voting public. We would meet the candidates free of filters, or prejudices of interpreters, or commentary of any kind. We would be able to directly hear and see the individual describing his ideas, ideas that would affect us should he hold office. The proposal for debates was for four consecutive Sundays leading up to and running right into when the general elections would be held, the second Tuesday in November.

The first response from the opposition candidate was that if the debates were held on these Sundays, on the suggested dates, they "would conflict with the televised playoff in the World Series games."

This is the first thing that a person who considers themselves qualified to be the leader of our nation thinks. Now without casting any judgement upon what the motives might be for that, to me it says something in a much more expanded way. This reflects a kind of consciousness, not only on this individual's part or in a political way, it reflects a consciousness that we are willing to live with in this country.

To compare the direct communication a debate would offer and what that means to us in terms of electing a president to represent us worldwide, to a baseball playoff as if they are of equal importance says a great deal about our society. About ourselves.

The second news item occurred within the same physical time

frame. This one also concerned sports. It involved an individual who is a basketball star. He is very good at what he does. He had worked as a professional in basketball in the U.S. until he was diagnosed with one of the raging illnesses of the day, acquired immune deficiency syndrome (AIDS). He retired, and was now renegotiating to get back into the game.

The announcement concerned this player signing the biggest monetary contract in the history of the sport. For playing a single season his salary would be 14.6 million dollars.

The sportscaster had done the math. He figured in an entire season, even if this player played every single minute of every game available in a season, that would mean this man would pocket $3600.00 every minute. Think about that.

Think about priorities and think about what is important in life. Think about the other piece of information you have in your brain. Think about your neighbor. At the least it points to a consciousness immersed in the material world.

There was a third article, a contemporary of these two, that ran in the *Kansas City Star*, a Midwestern paper. It listed comparative salaries for different positions in the community. Here we were told that the average beginning teacher's salary in Kansas City – the reimbursement for those who teach our children, the future leaders of our country – is $28,000 a year.

$14,600,000.00 a year to watch someone dribble and shoot a ball through a hoop compared with $28,000.00 to care for and enrich the minds of not just one child but twenty to forty minds a year!

Now consider this in light of the fact that one in eight people in the United States is illiterate.

When reasoners read these accounts they think about them because they are worthy of our time. Time we have because technology has freed us to think more deeply, more completely, more wholistically, about ourselves and our relationship with each other. These news items reflect a collective consciousness that assesses the worth of a profession such as teaching – the guiding of the mind, the body, the spirit of people – as a certain monetary amount. Then we assess the value of entertainment. We place a monetary value on sports performance.

The two don't even begin to balance.

It causes one to wonder about our awareness of who we are. It causes one to question our sense of values as a people, as souls. You begin to recognize the roots of mankind's restlessness is a spiritual hunger. It is not enough to believe in God. We need a revelation of God in man.

Although how we use our technology, the nervous system of the collective consciousness of the planet, may give us feedback we would rather ignore or deny, we must respond to it. Most souls during our early years have a certain kind of openness, an innocence, a sense of wonder about the world. You can experience this watching children. They chase a rainbow, seeking where it begins or ends. They are enthralled with a night sky filled with glittering stars and planets. You can watch a child listen to a chorus of birds, wondering where the music comes from. Children relish creation.

There is a spiritual nature. You can see a spirituality in the caress of a mother to a child or the steadying hand of a father or in the watchful eye of a sibling caring for a smaller brother or sister. You can see those threads of spirituality.

As we grow older, we physically mature but it almost seems like instead of blossoming spiritually we become more and more spiritually retarded. Stunted in our spiritual growth. It doesn't take very long, usually around the time of adolescence, for us to become involved with appearances. We become involved with comparing ourselves with other people. We try to keep up with other people, possessing the same things. We even compete with other people, trying to get better things.

This attitude grows and continues into our physical adult years. Its as if the consciousness remains in the adolescent thinking patterns even as the body ages.

More and more materiality becomes important and our spirituality fades. In time we find that it is position, or possessions, or it is money, or it is time that becomes our God. That is a seed of consciousness that will accept some of these things that I noted earlier.

The things of the material become so important your spirituality is still there but it is not part of the consciousness.

To have God revealed to you and in your life, requires an expansion of your consciousness. Your thinking must change. Your attitudes must rearrange. You cannot be the same as you are today. You must learn to breathe, to move to be with God.

Growing in God awareness requires a living concept of the Creator that affects your thinking, that will be in your thoughts, that will influence your daily conduct. You can draw inspiration from this thriving concept for you have found it to be universally true. When you strive for that kind of consciousness, that kind of spirituality, God lives in your life and you become a channel through which God can be seen, can be heard, can be felt, can be tasted, can be touched by other people.

To attain that consciousness requires dedication. Every Holy scripture of the world speaks of meditation as a means to reveal God. *The Yaznas,* part of the *Zend Avesta,* the teachings of Zarathustra, the great Persian Master, convey this idea:

> *"This I ask thee, O Lord Ahura. Instruct me so that I may ponder thy revelations and understand the good mind within me. Give guidance that I might attain through thine order to life's perfection. Let me know how my soul with joyfulness may increase in goodness."*

This embodies not only a thought, but as it permeates your consciousness it becomes an attitude. The truth of these words, their meaning, becomes a part of your existence, a part of your being so that with every breath you take you exude this kind of awareness. Life is to relish and to perfect. It is time to create.

It is an opportunity to shine the goodness that you have within, without.

There are three movements of consciousness that universally elevate consciousness to reveal God thus initiating, quickening, and bringing about spiritual renaissance.

The first is stilling the mind.

Your mind can be populated with so many thoughts. If your attention is scattered, you leave yourself at the whim and mercy of any number of disturbing thoughts, attachments, and unruly ideas. A state of mental relaxation becomes the object of your desire. Mental relaxation is characterized by being able to give your undivided attention at will to one thing at a time or to one subject at a time. This is the beginning of understanding what stilling the mind is.

If you practice meditation you know that stilling the mind is prerequisite to enjoying communion with your Creator.

There is a wonderful parable from Zen Buddhist teachings that describes eloquently stilling the mind.

It is said that a most intelligent man once came to the Zen Master Nannin seeking answers to the mystery of life. Being a professor of philosophy, the man's queries about God and meditation were endless. The master listened in silence.

When the man had temporarily exhausted his requests, the master said, "You look tired. Having climbed this high mountain and traveled to this far away place. Come and rest, while I prepare you tea."

Although his mind boiled with questions, the professor waited while the tea brewed. As its rich aroma filled the room the Master said, "Be patient. Don't be in such a hurry. Who knows? Even by drinking tea, your questions may be answered."

At this the professor began to doubt the wisdom of the teacher. He began wondering if his entire journey had been a waste of time. This man seems mad, he thought. What do my questions about God and the divine have to do with tea? Yet the professor was indeed tired, as the master had perceived, and if he was soon to descend this mount he needed refreshment.

The Master brought the kettle, poured the tea in the cup and the tea started overflowing into the saucer. The professor was startled by the clumsiness and amazed when the master continued to allow the tea to flow until the saucer also was filled. Just one more drop and the tea would start flowing onto the table and the floor.

The professor exclaimed, "Stop! What are you doing! Can't you see the cup is full and the saucer is full?"

Nannin replied, "That is the exact condition you find yourself in.

"Your mind is so full of questions that even if I answer, you don't have any space to receive the wisdom. Since you entered this palace, your questions have overflowed. This small abode is filled with your questions.

"Return from whence you came, empty your cup and then come. If you are to fulfill your desire to know the great mysteries of life, you must first create a space for them to enter."

Stilling your mind is essential for communion. It is very difficult to have communion, to have a conversation, whether it is with God or a friend, when there is no time of stilling your mind. For communion, there must be a time of receiving what the other has to give. Stilling the mind is essential to those seeking the revelation of God.

The next step is daily communion with God. And this is the actual endeavor, once the mind is stilled, to accomplish that we call meditation.

Man has hypnotized himself to believe he is a human being. You are not a human being. You are a soul and your essence is spirit. You begin to know and live this truth as you reveal God in your consciousness and your life.

Meditation is the time and space you make daily for God in your life.

There are many purposes for meditation. One of them is greater awareness of who you are and your purpose for existence. To be able to experience complete joy and peace is a reason to meditate. To have a greater sense of caring about yourself and other people is also a reason to meditate. To revitalize your mind, your body, and your spirit is a benefit of meditation.

Through meditation you receive answers to your prayers.

Your prayers are an integral part of your well-being. Through every religion in the world there is a form of prayer that is taught. There is also a form of meditation that is to become a part of worship and devotional practices. They are often presented as two separate disciplines. Uniting the two initiates Spiritual Renaissance.

Prayer is aggressive. Prayer is the capacity to state what you desire. Meditation is the skilled, stilling of the mind to receive an answer. A feedback to whatever your prayer is. The qualities of your prayers are very important. You must learn the art of asking the right questions if you expect to receive the right answers. The right questions are part of the prayer you create.

There is another story I'd like to share with you about prayer that I found personally, as a teacher, insightful, and perhaps you will derive inspiration as well.

It is said that one of the great spiritual Masters, Moses, once came upon a man who was praying. The man's prayer sounded so strange that Moses stopped.

As he listened, he realized the man's prayer was insulting to God.

"Let me come close to you," the man prayed, "and I promise to clean your body when it is dirty. If lice are there, I will take them away. And I am a good shoemaker. I will make you perfect shoes.

"Nobody looks after your needs Lord. I will make sure your needs are met. If you fall ill, I will serve you and bring to you what will cleanse you of sickness. I know how to cook and I will prepare lavish feasts of nourishment for you."

Enraged, Moses interrupted the man shouting, "Stop! Stop! You heresy. What are you saying? That God has lice on his body? That God's clothes are dirty and that you will clean them? That God can be ill and have need for food that you will cook for him? Who taught you this prayer?"

Stunned, the man tearfully replied, "No one taught me this prayer. I have not learned it from anywhere. I am very poor and I am very uneducated and I don't know how to pray. I have made it up from the things I know.

"Life troubles me very much, so it must trouble God.

Sometimes the food I find is not very good and my stomach aches. God must also suffer in this way sometimes. This is just my own experience that has become my prayer, but if you know the right prayer please teach me."

Filled with compassion, Moses taught the man the right prayer. The man bowed down to Moses, thanking him as tears of deep gratitude flowed from his eyes. The man departed and Moses was very pleased at this opportunity to help another to see his error and learn the correct way to pray.

While Moses slept, God appeared to him in a dream. His voice filled with anger, God said, "I sent you there to bring people closer to me but now you have thrown away one of my greatest lovers. This right prayer you have taught him will keep him from me. He will now only repeat the words you have told him.

"Those words will be a barrier between his spirit and mine. It is not a prayer at all.

"Prayer has nothing to do with law. Prayer is the love. Love is a law onto itself. It needs no other law.

"Know that my servant, with love comes grace. With love comes truth. Truth is the liberation of the spirit."

Our prayers are important in meditation.

Prayers can be topical. You can pray about hope or courage or love or wisdom or forgiveness.

Prayers can be a query. "How can I be more compassionate with my loved one?" "How can I control my emotions?" "How can I accept change more readily?"

They can reflect a desire for communion with your God, "Dear God, I want to know you. I want to exist with you. I want to be like you."

They can be thanksgiving prayers, acknowledging what you have received. These prayers transform your consciousness, because they elevate your consciousness from the taking of one who is unworthy to appreciating being a son or daughter of the Creator.

Your prayers are valid. What matters is that your prayer comes from your heart. And your mind. When your prayer comes from your heart and mind, you draw closer to your God. You experience the communion for which you even take the time to meditate.

Once we still the mind and once we experience daily communion with God, we are prepared for the next step of the revelation of God in man. This is living meditatively.

In practice this is for most the greatest challenge. You will attain times of stilling your mind. You can discipline yourself so that every day, without fail, you spend a specific length of physical time in meditation. To truly live meditatively is a scientific art because it brings the benefit of a stilled consciousness of one who has communed with God into every waking moment.

Living meditatively is the blossoming of spirituality in your existence. It is constant awareness of yourself as spirit, each day. It renews and revitalizes.

There is a parable about a disciple who had been practicing spiritual discipline for some time.

Having reached a pinnacle in his efforts, and feeling unable to move further on the path, he sought the guidance and instruction of a Master Teacher. He arrived at the Master's abode amid a furious storm. Before he entered the house, the disciple left his shoes and umbrella outside so they would not soil the domain.

Following introductions, the Master asked the disciple,

"On which side of your shoes did you leave your umbrella?"

The disciple thought, this is a curious question. He expected one who had achieved mastery to speak of divine matters. To the disciple's mind the Master should be talking about God, about the Kundalini rising, about Buddha, about chakras opening. And life happening in your head. But this so-called Master was concerned with the most mundane of events.

The Disciple was at a loss and somewhat perturbed. What did shoes and umbrellas have to do with spirituality? How could they compare with the pain he experienced in his present spiritual stagnation?

Asking the questions again, the Master directed the disciple's attention to his query.

The disciple reflected. Finally he could not remember and could not answer. Who would bother to remember on which side he had placed an umbrella, he thought in disgust.

Failing to answer, the Master refused to instruct the disciple saying, "Then go and meditate for seven more years."

"Seven years!" the disciple exclaimed. His mind divided by anger born of rejection, and pity born from pain, his mind immediately filled with thoughts of punishment for such a small mistake. Thinking he might sway the Master to see how unreasonable He was being, the disciple said, "I must leave and meditate for seven more years just for this small fault?"

"Faults are not small or big," replied the Master.

"You are just not yet living meditatively.

"You see, when you live meditatively you know how to still your mind. If you know how to still your mind, you know how to concentrate. You can remember where you put your shoes and where you put your umbrella. You remember that

where you put your shoes and where you put your umbrella is just such an act of creation, of spirituality, as praying. Or as meditating."

The insights gained in meditation need to fill your consciousness. They need to become part of your existence and your essence. So no matter where you are and no matter what you are doing, whether you are at peace or in turmoil, whether you are happy or you are angry, you still have the essence of living meditatively.

The *Koran* counsels us to bear God in mind at all times. I think that is what it is to live meditatively.

Part of the awareness born from stilling the mind, meditating, and bringing the spiritual fruits into your everyday life is realizing the beauty of the physical world. This enlightened perspective becomes part of your existence, your consciousness. It guides the way you view events and happenings around and within you. It determines the way you read newspapers, the way you hear conversations, the way you greet a stranger.

You realize that the physical world is in truth a schoolroom, a place for learning. You realize you are here to learn and to teach, to give and to receive, as is each other person. As is each part of creation. This awareness is constant.

You also realize that although you live in a material world, you are not the physical body you inhabit. Rather you, the Real Self as the Hindu teachings counsel, are a soul incarned for spiritual refinement and progression. The more you reveal God in your consciousness, you know who you are and who you are meant to be.

Old thoughts are past. A fresher realization of yourself as spirit begins to permeate your dealings with self and others. You begin to live up to your ideals never doubting the importance of the path you have chosen. Whatever that path may be.

In living up to your ideals you embody creation itself.

In this way, the Creator is reflected in you.

The people you associate with, the places you frequent, the things that you use in your experiences, choose with care. They are the people, the places, and the things that will assist you in your journey toward enlightenment. You clothe yourself in these.

All others you leave behind you. They pass away.

To live meditatively, you don't ever embrace something that is going to hinder the progression of your soul. Or the realization of your consciousness.

You begin to love in a manner that transcends physical conditions and emotional attachments. As you do so in your everyday, waking life you are preparing yourself to receive ever-greater awareness of the love of your Creator. The love of the Creator is not emotional. It is not attachment. It is not physical.

The *Analects* of Confucius says:

> *"Exert yourself to achieve your proper merit.*
>
> *In giving heed to the beginning, think of the end. Then the end will be without distress.*
>
> *God will lead men to tranquil security. Seek to be in harmony with all your neighbors. Live in amenity with all your neighbors. Tranquilize and serve others."*

This embodies the attitude of one who lives meditatively. They are self aware, not self absorbed. They are constantly as acutely aware of you and your needs, as they ever are of their own for they realize a uniting of consciousness that only comes through stilling the mind through meditation and through living meditatively.

When we collectively conceive the Creator, so the awareness of the presence of God is omnipresent, society will change. It will evolve. What it values will reflect more God-consciousness.

You will know you are experiencing revelation when God is

present in the satisfaction of a want, in the dealings with other people and with ourselves, in reading a book or in conversation, in doing a daily task or in meditation, even in times of sorrow and times of gladness. When our conception of God is within us, alive, then we have expanded our consciousness to reveal God.

As the *Dhammapada* counsels,

> *"There is no meditation apart from wisdom.*
>
> *"There is no wisdom apart from meditation.*
>
> *"Those in whom wisdom and meditation meet are not far from Nirvana."*

Now we were a nation obsessed with immediate gratification – can't wait til Monday, must have that album, dress, fax, wine, ticket, man, woman, child, today – now!

What would happen if we had the same emergency toward our Maker – can't wait til tomorrow, I must pray, meditate, talk to God, feel his presence, now!

When your mind is filled with Godly matters there is no room for anything less.

Sunday

It hasn't been that long since the same was true every Sunday in America.

No ringing of cash registers. Only the steady stream of men, women, and children going to church or temple. Then coming home to enjoy each other's company, or gathering at a relative's for a big Sunday dinner.

Slowly America lost its tranquility in a sea of physical temptation. Greed for sensory satisfaction replaced a yearning for spiritual communion. And the so-called blue laws fell one by one as if the rules a society of people lived by never existed at all. Now anything could happen on Sunday. The laws became the victim of adolescent banter. Those who upheld them, the subject of arrogant scorn. It was no longer fashionable to be devout, to be faithful meant you were naive.

Once there was a time in America when you couldn't buy or sell on Sunday. It was God's day. You rested, just as God rested from creating on the seventh day. Everyone knew it, even unbelievers.

Most didn't know how close such a simple act of reverence could bring you to your Maker. Trying to be like God did place God in your consciousness, at least for a day.

What most people did know was you weren't supposed to lie, cheat, steal, fornicate or murder on any day. But it was especially offensive on Sunday. Even those with a propensity to hurt others knew it.

Hasn't been that many years ago when the small towns - even Buffalo, Missouri the town with the smallest Walmart in the world - accepted manmade laws that took God's day from him.

Eccentric, you say. Fanatic, you think. If we ask God's favor so often should we not be willing to favor him?

Shouldn't "Do unto others as you would have them do unto you" apply first to how we "do" with our own Maker?

The Chinese have a proverb for those who fail to give due reverence, "Those who offend the gods have no one to whom to pray."

When America stopped honoring the Sabbath it did more than violate one of the ten commandments. As once remarked, they are the ten commandments, not the ten suggestions.

When America made Sunday a day like any other day, it did something ignoble. This was not removing an offense to a very few citizens, the secular idea of separating church and state. This was America lowering its standards, progeny misinterpreting *The Constitution* that binds us together to favor the selfishness which will always tear us apart.

We hid our spiritual rebellion by making ourselves believe we were not rejecting a Heavenly Father, rather we were fighting men, the founding fathers of our nation. Who were they and what did they know anyway? They lived two hundred years ago, things are different now, we need change.

The truth is when America made Sunday a day like every other day, it collectively banished its ideal.

No longer were we a nation under God, willing to sacrifice our lives for a just cause. Now we were a nation obsessed with immediate gratification – can't wait til Monday, must have that album, dress, fax, wine, ticket, man, woman, child, today – now!

What would happen if we had the same emergency toward our Maker – can't wait til tomorrow, I must pray, meditate, talk to God, feel his presence, now!

When your mind is filled with Godly matters there is no room for anything less. Lying stops. Stealing stops. Lust ends. So do thieving, adultery, murder.

Yes, we have made it easier for man to experience and create by claiming Sunday for our own self-important purposes. It no longer belongs to God and we can now do anything we please. Aye, there's the rub. In the process of demanding freedom the pleasure has eluded us.

Sunday is just another day to work, to make money. Political programs have replaced televised Sunday services that brought the spirit of God to shut-ins and the sick. Even sports events, a kick when you win but a common excuse for spouse and child abuse for the losers. There is no pleasure there, only pain.

We have forgotten, or worse never experienced, what it is that pleases. A restless consciousness misses the Truth that brings real joy. A child's smile. The warmth of the sun on your face. The aroma of springtime flowers. The touch of your friend's hand. A neighbor's supportive good wishes or helping hand in a time of need.

Many do not even know that what is missing in their lives is not a person they have yet to meet or enough money to buy a position in society.

What is missing is Sunday. Those days, those hours, devoted to spiritual consciousness.

What is missing are Sundays where, at the least, you wondered what would motivate the storeowner to stay home and lose your business. Those Sundays where, at the most, you sought the inspiration you needed to live a better life through your work; to be a better person for your family, friends, and community.

There was a time when most Americans knew that Spiritual consciousness brings order to life. We believed in things greater than ourselves, and so we accomplished great things.

When we as a nation took time for our Creator, we were affirming our need for deeper understanding, for excellence beyond our present capacity, for wisdom we hoped to someday gain, for meta-physical matters. This freedom of consciousness was the American dream of our founding fathers – Self mastery, Self destiny.

At first only those providing God's service worked on Sundays – ministers, priests, doctors and nurses, firemen and policemen. Their willingness to serve was a testimony to the reality of God. Then came the vendors, like moneychangers in a temple, those providing services not a matter of life and death but a matter of greed or sacrifice for both seller and buyer. And along with the moneychangers went the heart of the American Dream. Acquire and possess replaced aspire and progress.

Perhaps through our experiences we can now release the bonds of physical thinking. Perhaps now we can admit the power of faith and let go the chains of greed. In Truth it is faith that controls the living, living that brings the having.

It is worth considering the restoration of God's day.

Afterall the ten commandments are going on their third millennia. They are expressions of the Universal Laws and Truths which govern our existence as human beings. We will do well to acquaint ourselves with them and endeavor to live in harmony with them. Whenever we do so we are richly rewarded. We find peace of mind.

We live peaceably because we are thinking peacefully.

Restoring Sunday to its former place of respectability and dignity can heal any American wound. It will open the eye to what is divine and attune the inner ear to a higher calling. It will challenge the mind to learn and grow. It will soften the heart toward greater understanding while strengthening the will to pursue it. It is the Sabbath we are resurrecting. The Lord's Day. The Holiest of all Holy Days. A day of peace.

A common action which brings us home one day each week will rekindle the Dream for one generation while it brings the Dream to a new one. America can reclaim its place as leader of a free world. We can initiate a spiritual revival that transforms the consciousness of everyone on Earth.

Let us again seek as a society to commune with our Maker and with each other. Let us embrace Godly matters again, no longer fearing His influence in our lives. Let us reestablish divine communication inviting Him into our homes and work places.

Let us make sacred covenants that enable us to live with ourselves. For that is what will prepare us for the next millennium. That is what will empower us, in the words of Tennyson, to "Ring out the 1000 years of war. Ring in the 1000 years of peace."

Then perhaps spiritual consciousness will reign in the minds and hearts of us all and everyday will be Sunday.

XI

The Spiritual Renaissance

Communion

*"When the Great Tao prevailed,
the world was a commonwealth;
men of talent and virtue were selected,
mutual confidence was emphasized,
and brotherhood was cultivated.
Therefore, men did not regard as parents
only their own parents,
nor did they treat as sons only their own sons.
Old people were able to enjoy their old age;
young men were able to employ their talents,
juniors respected their elders;
helpless widows, orphans, and cripples were well cared for.
Men had their respective occupations,
and women their homes.
They hated to see wealth lying about in waste,
and they did not hoard it for their own use.
They hated not to use their energies,
and they used their energies not for their own benefit.
Thus evil schemings were repressed,
and robbers, thieves, and traitors no longer appeared,
so that the front door remained open.
This was called the Ta-tung (Grant Unity)."*

- Confucius, Chinese moral teacher (550-478 B.C.)

Spiritual Communion

The End to All Secrets

Throughout the history of mankind there have been schools of thought that have taught the development of consciousness throughout the ages. They have been secretive. They have been cloistered in Himalayan monasteries or the halls of the Vatican. They have been specialized as was the school of Pythagorus and Aristotle's Academy.

The ancient wisdom has only been available to an elite group, not the masses. You either gained admittance through birth, or through money, or through position, or place on the earth where you were born, or you were appointed to it.

How inspiring that such is not the case with the education the School of Metaphysics offers. You are not appointed to it. You don't have to have a lot of money. You don't have to be born into it. It is openly available to anyone and each individual comes to it, chooses it, because his heart leads him there.

I first came to a School of Metaphysics class as a favor to a friend. Or so I initially thought.

As we entered the one-bedroom apartment where the class was held, I had no inkling of how my life was about to change. Far beyond the ragings of my uncontrolled imagination - "Are you sure this is where the class is? Who else is supposed to be here? Do you know these people?" - was the reality of the adventure I was embarking upon.

Like heroes and heroines I had read about in the world's myths, I was in the most unlikely place, at an unanticipated time, meeting my destiny. I had no idea that on that hot summer day, July 1, 1975, I would start down a road that would challenge my intellect, call upon my reasoning, spark my genius, cultivate my intuition, inspire my divinity.

I am increasingly grateful I did.

I also had yet to discover that this study would challenge what I had previously learned about life. Far from asking me to discard or ignore early teachings, this course in what causes our physical world to exist expected me to draw upon what I had learned. It expected me to use the truths of what I had been taught - whether at home, school, church, marketplace, or social circles - and to add to my awareness of truth for personal excellence.

This study would prove to be unlike any I had known.

It would in time remind me of previous schooling. For instance, as a child I had learned a language to communicate ideas, now I was learning a Universal Language that would enable me to communicate with anyone on the planet and most importantly with my own inner self. I had learned to commit millions of bits of information to memory - colors, shapes, numbers, names of trees, birds, countries, planets, governments, rulers, dates, places, on and on - and now I was learning how to access that memory at will. I had learned that many uses of my imagination were respected and encouraged, some even earning admiration and praise, but I thought my imagination was a gift from God and therefore responsive to his desire, not necessarily my own. I didn't know imagination too is a skill that can be developed through practice. Now I was learning how to employ that creative skill to imagine something different, something better.

I had learned early in life what to think. "Basics" akin to those noted in every good sermon: be good, be kind, think well of others, be loyal, be trustworthy, have and display common sense, look out after others welfare, stand up for what you believe in, do the right thing. I had lived long enough to realize sometimes it was difficult to live up to those ideals. Honesty was a highly prized trait but which should one choose: telling the truth when you know it will hurt another or refraining from telling that truth, the lie of omission, to spare them hurt? My life was filled with paradoxes and conundrums such as this.

I didn't know that first night of class that this study in metaphysics was going to teach me what I had longed to know: truth that would set me free.

Metaphysics, I learned, is a study based upon Truths that are universal. Truths that apply to anyone, anywhere, anytime. Truths that operate in our lives independent of our knowledge or acceptance of them and indifferent to our wealth or physical influence.

One by one these Truths set me free to understand the many whys in my life: why one person dies in a plane crash while the person next to them does not, why children are born deformed, why man continues to repeat history's mistakes over and over again, why people can justify killing in the name of God, why a truly good person can have horror enter their life while a truly evil person can escape the responsibility of being judged. These Truths set me free to learn, understand, and grow in wisdom.

Little did I know at the time that I had begun a personal quest for Enlightenment.

The kind of education that promotes and encourages Enlightenment is what every soul yearns for. Expanded consciousness is what ultimately every soul will achieve. The beauty of the School of Metaphysics is that it is designed for those who want to accelerate their evolution.

This school exists for the people who are not satisfied with waiting. They are not the kind of person who tends toward procrastination, they do not just wait and see what happens. This education is for the kind of person who wants to make things happen, who has a vision for the future, and an image of what it means to be enlightened. Such a person emulates Great Masters they have read about, or indeed known, sincerely wanting to be like those people. Such an aspirant desires to be close to his God. He wants to be able to give back to humanity just some of what he has received in lifetime after lifetime after lifetime.

When this type of person is a child, he or she is described as talented and gifted. I became familiar with the real needs of these children years ago when we sponsored a project called Clean Up America. Each year we gave one hundred percent of the money collected for the project to schools for talented and gifted children.

We met with unexpected challenges. With a nation that affords all of its youth a basic education, you would believe we would also respond to the accelerated needs of the future leaders, inventors, visionaries, and explorers. Originally, when we started looking, we found all kinds of schools and programs for what were called "special" kids, children mentally or physically impaired. This was not the case for the quick learners. Schools for the talented and gifted were rare and programs often consisted of one hour a week of studies different from the regular curriculum.

The shocking truth was few people knew enough about *how* to learn to adequately teach these young minds. This is so important because what happens in the first seven years of our lives lays the foundation, the pattern, for an entire lifetime. These patterns are repeated throughout the life over and over. The strengths as well as the weaknesses. This does not mean that you can't overcome any kind of adversity that you may experience as a young child. It does mean that what we give a newly incarned soul during the first seven years will make or break that individual for that lifetime.

Applying metaphysical principles and practices in your own life prepares you for parenting. When you know basics of disciplining the mind, you can teach them to a child. Concentration, listening, recall, meditation, relaxation, intuitive skills. Personal responsibility, integrity, wisdom, and a love for Truth. When you learn spiritual principles and practices from a very young age, you can imagine what you might be able to accomplish throughout an entire lifetime.

How *and* what we teach the youth of the world determines the kind of world we will know in the next ten years, fifty years, the next hundred years. A recent U.S. survey of kindergarten through twelfth grade teachers asked what skills they thought their students would absolutely need in the next millennium. About 45% of them said the students would need a second language, mastery of a second language. About 63% said they would need science and math skills. Sixty-seven percent said that students would need to have technology and information background, which I interpreted as computer skills.

What is most revealing is what the teachers agreed upon: 95% said their students would need proficiency in *problem solving*. Yet, very little problem solving is being taught in U.S. schools. Yes, there is a bevy of hypothetical "what if's" but these are nothing more than secularized morality plays that teach our youth how to think negatively. They fail to teach reasoning which is the instrument of problem solving.

Imagination is being taught even less in our schools. We can continue to wait till a problem arises, then go about using our innate or "God-given" reasoning capacities to try to correct it. But it's far more visionary to be able to imagine what you want to occur that will benefit yourself and other people then find a way to make it happen. The difference is feast or famine. The difference is peace or war. The difference is wealth or poverty.

If you have to wait for conditions to be a problem, then you have to wait for famine. You have to wait for poverty. You have to wait for sickness. You have to wait for war before you can set the creative intelligence on peace, you may die before you have the opportunity to do so. We must teach our children how to use their minds fully, productively.

As a nation, as a planet, we must admit that education is not just learning how to read and write, although these are very important. Education is learning the mechanics of how thinking occurs because once you learn that, you can do anything. That is freedom, and that's why I've spent twenty years teaching metaphysics. I could have taught many things. I could have chosen to specialize in writing or in art or in some kind of physical endeavor. But I would not have been as influential because what I teach people here is the key to being able to have anything you desire.

I know every time I teach someone how to use his mind effectively, I have opened every door in the universe to him. All he has to do is choose which one he wants to walk through. This is the essence of education in the next millennium. It is the kind of education that will help make the Spiritual Renaissance a reality.

The world needs many spiritual teachers. Older, wiser souls must be willing to mentor younger, hungry souls, inviting the inner consciousness to come forward.

The School of Metaphysics has been preparing people to meet this challenge by studying, researching, living and teaching the development of consciousness. The wholistic education being revealed is a forerunner in uniting that which very much divides people in the world today. The two groups can most readily be described as people of a religious nature and those of a scientific persuasion. A chasm stands between the two and they seem never to agree. They are constantly at odds. The beauty of metaphysical study, and the application of causal principles, causes the mind to transcend whatever differences or conflicts there might be between science and religion.

It begins very simply, building upon the unlimited potential of the individual. *Memory. Imagination. Attention.* Each of these mental skills are taught, learned and strengthened. We, at the School of Metaphysics, teach adults how to use the power of their minds. We know one's command of reasoning determines the quality of his life, success or failure, solitary or companioned, memorable or forgettable. It also dictates whether he is happy or sad, friendly or adversarial, at peace or in turmoil. A reasoner can rise above his original station in life. History is filled with such people. And now it is time for more of them, many more. The time is coming when the outstanding leader, the scientific inventor, the artistic genius, and yes the spiritual master, will no longer be the minority. The time is approaching for humankind to experience a surgence of creative genius that will initiate an era of Enlightenment yet to be seen on this planet. This will require changes in education and in religion.

In the present educational system there are all kinds of attempts to instill in our youth and the youth of America concepts like respect. Respect for diversity, respect for other's points of view. Respect for opinions. This is pervasive, not only in how we educate our youth but in how we live our own lives. The media reports and promotes the concept daily. They'll say "arguably" the most important factor to longevity, "arguably" the best restaurant in town, "arguably" the smartest candidate for presidency. Listen for it, you'll hear it. It's always "arguably". Nobody stands for what they believe in anymore. This is a result of the idea and how it's been promoted of "respecting someone else's opinion." It's difficult to teach something you know nothing about it. It's very difficult to teach respect when you don't teach concentration. From being able to focus your mind, you can understand what something is. Once you understand something, you can pay your respects. When this understanding is lacking, in place of respect you find fear. And what do we see in too many of our schools? We see children who are scared to go to school. We find teachers who are scared to go to school. Why? Because of drugs, because of guns, because of the threats of violence.

Imagine, what will happen when we teach children how to focus the power of their mind. What will happen when we encourage them to imagine rather than wait for a problem to solve? What will happen when we teach them to meditate; to find a place of peace within themselves? Where there's love, where there's peace, where there's generosity, where there's hope, there is no place for fear or hatred or anger or destruction. This is universally true. In many ways, in the educational system in this country, we have tried to secularize concepts that traditionally have been religious. We have tried to separate what we call church and state. When what the country was founded upon was a freedom to be able to express your sense of spirituality. Your sense of religion whatever it might be. It is freedom *of* religion, not freedom *from* religion. We find ourselves in a quandary, needing the spirit of the law while denying the spirit exists.

And so we come back to the School of Metaphysics because the School of Metaphysics goes where no government and no educational system has gone before. It marches right in the middle of teaching spirituality. Not as a belief system or as a dogma, but as a series of spiritual and mental disciplines that open the individual to genius, to the supernatural, to the divine. These disciplines that are based upon universal principles apply to anyone, anytime, anywhere. It does not matter what color you are, it doesn't matter how tall or short, it does not matter how rich or poor, it does not matter if you are well or ill, it does not matter which country you are born in, it doesn't matter what religion you follow. You can become a metaphysician. You can access the levels of your own consciousness. And from that, your entire life will be enriched.

I remember vividly when I received the sixth lesson in metaphysics studies, which is centered on friendship, my thoughts reached to combine early religious training with the friends I had at the time. Did I really have to be hurt or disappointed when a friend broke a date? Was I being spiritual when I held a grudge because of an unkind word or broken promise? I could let go, after all I was the one hurt the most by the resentment. I had not realized this before. I was only beginning to realize the power within me.

What did it mean to "do unto others as I would have them do unto me?" How could I bring the truth I saw into my dealings with others.

This became increasingly important to me because the way I related with others was constantly changing as my thinking was expanding. I found myself wanting to meditate rather than stay up past midnight repeating a conversation we had had two hours before. I had ceased indulging in mind-altering substances when I started classes, and was finding the friendships with those who continued to imbibe weakening. If asked at the time why our paths separated I would have said, we just don't have anything in common anymore.

I realized with Lesson Six the true import of what this meant and why it was so important. Time was becoming more valuable to me. My old friends were still looking for ways to pass the time. I'd always had a sense that time was rapidly slipping through my fingers. Now, I had the tools to give meaning to time. I no longer wanted to indulge in activities I considered a waste of time. As my learning accelerated I drew friendships with people of like mind to me. New opportunities for caring, sharing, loving.

Love had always been important to me, and now I had

license to explore, discover, and live. I wanted to love completely, without condition, and as long as I was willing to look I could recognize and make improvement in this area. What a difference this made and continues to make in my life. I am progressively freer to express my ideas, to give love and compliments and praise. I can tell the truth, rather than hide it for fear of another's rejection or personal dislike. I have learned as much about letting go as I have about embracing.

What I am able to do, as I deeply consider thought provoking ideas such as these, is transform more than my relationships with others, more than my thinking, I transform *me*. So many awarenesses have changed the way I see myself and the world. I have defused issues that, left unresolved, would have produced unhappiness all my life. Arising from limited understanding of life experiences, questions like "why did my mother try to become part of my circle of friends when I was a teenager," "why did the love of my high school-college years suddenly choose homosexuality," "why did I fall ill every April" haunted me, begging for attention that I at last knew how to give. They were secret fears and pains and longings, echoing in my consciousness bringing insecurity and self-doubt.

Learning to ask the right questions freed me to discover some startling answers to problems like these. My consciousness moved into spaces where understanding reigned and generosity flowed. I reached a new heighth in experiencing love. When I learned how to respect my parents as people first, acceptance naturally followed. I didn't have to work at it. It was a matter of cause and effect. When I learned how previous existences are relative to the present, concerning both mental and physical heredity, I could understand the narcisstic attachment that holds people back. When I learned the connection between ways of thinking and the function of the physical body, health was in my hands. Self realization forms the kind of person I am, the kind of spouse and parent I am, the kind of leader I am.

By posing the quintessential questions - *where did I come from? where am I going? why am I here? and who am I?* - I understand how students are asked to stretch their minds in this course of study. They must reach into the storehouse of knowledge gleaned through their lives. To come to reasonable conclusions they must draw upon what experience has taught them about life and love and being and destiny. In this way they transcend the limited experience of one and elevate their awareness to what is universally true.

This greatest secret known to mankind is daily being revealed to me. To align your waking thoughts with that which is universally true for all people, is to realize compassion. As Emerson described it, *"To know that what you believe to be true is true for all men, – that is genius."* When your grasp of truth is the universal, you are connected with all people. You know your Creator.

If it sounds religious that's because it is, in the truest definition of the word. For years I've taught people that metaphysical study makes your religion more real to you, it does not take you away from your religion. I am more a Christian, in the true sense of the word, now than I have been in my entire life. Muslims and Buddhists I have taught say the same about their religion.

Free to move beyond the confines of dogma, I have come to know the richness in the religious Holy scriptures of the world. I draw from them for my own enlightenment as well as to inspire others toward enlightenment. This kind of openness comes with developing your own consciousness. You quickly realize the more expanded your consciousness, the more we have in common. When you leave behind small-mindedness you realize how small the world is.

Interconnectedness, unity born from enlightenment, is what the School of Metaphysics is bringing to the world. In a secular sense, schooling focused on cultivating genius, education centered on *how* to learn instead of *what* to learn, is unique in today's world. In a religious vein, schooling devoted to the Enlightenment of Spirit is virtually nonexistent for most. Opportunities to learn are far too rare.

As the Spiritual Renaissance approaches what has for ages been secret will be made known. Prophecies will be fulfilled in ways previously unimagined. Revelation will become an increasing part of all of our lives.

It is time for man to move beyond believing into a state of knowing.

We believe, and from our research we know, that you can teach someone how to realize Self as soul. This has until now been solely religious territory. Science avoids the issue. Eastern faiths do not address the existence of soul. For most Westerners soul is a concept, a result of faith. It's something you believe exists — somewhere. You hope that your soul will be saved from any kind of punishment or purgatory or hell or damnation in the future because you live a good life. This is the extent to which most people go in their thinking. This is the commonly-accepted Western view of the soul.

A metaphysician thinks beyond the norm, embracing bold insights that bring new awarenesses to mankind. Metaphysicians recognize that they are a soul and that the physical body is a temporary form the soul inhabits. They realize the physical conditions of their lives are transient, coming and going in a constant state of change. They only exist in as much as the soul needs to learn. From this vantage point, the physical world becomes the soul's university, offering the opportunity to learn.

Learning — or more appropriately understanding — is the sole reason for the soul to assume physical form. It is the height of understanding for someone to identify with the soul, to know what the soul needs, and to be about the work that the soul has to do in order to become whole.

Most people's recognition of the soul is through dreams—their nighttime dreams. Far too many people don't pay attention to their dreams at all. Many people say, "I don't dream." When in reality, what they mean is "I don't remember dreaming." Scientifically we know that dreams occur in cycles every time we sleep.

Some people have access to their soul or recognize their soul in telepathic experiences. They think of something and the person that they are with says it out loud. Or they have a kind of rapport with a best friend or spouse; one person starts a sentence and the other one ends it. This kind of mind to mind communication, or telepathic rapport, is one expression of the soul.

Some people commune with departed loved ones or angels or other entities that exist beyond physical vibratory creation. Others have inklings or clairvoyant experiences perceive probabilities that indeed occur. Then there are those whose talent propels them far beyond the accepted boundaries of the average. Such proteges harmonize with inner resources and draw upon considerable wealth of wisdom to make everyone's life easier. These are ways that some people understand and know their soul.

Any intuitive faculty is a way for you to access your soul and therefore *know* that it exists. However for most people esoteric knowledge is left to chance. It comes and it goes seemingly on its own whim and without any kind of direction or any kind of understanding on the part of the individual. The course of study in the School of Metaphysics changes your fate. You are no longer at the mercy of some kind of force that is beyond your understanding and control.

Through spiritual discipline you begin to bring into your domain the understanding of the nature of your own consciousness.

The limitless power in it. And the awesome responsibility of it. You begin to recognize yourself not only as a soul but also as a spirit. Not only as a child of a God, or a Creator or a The Source, but as one who is maturing and trying to reach compatibility with that Maker. This is the kind of education that will become increasingly in demand in the years ahead.

I can look back on those days during that first year of my study, recalling them so keenly I can again see as I did, hear as I did, feel as I did. I bask in the warmth of their glow and timbre to their excitement. I was learning to live the ten commandments as positive guidelines to peace and contentment. I was learning that those same guidelines appear around the world in Holy scriptures. I was secretly thrilled that I now knew of ways to be closer to the Master I had learned about at my parent's knee, the one called Jesus of Nazareth. I had wanted to be like Christlike, to be wise, from the time I was young, and now I was understanding why.

When one of the founders of SOM pointed to the front door of the School and said, *"Someday through that door will walk a Christ,"* I silently hoped I might have the honor of being his or her metaphysics teacher. I was overwhelmed by my own boldness of thought, but I did not shy away from the secret thought that immediately welled up in response to his words. Rather I committed myself to endeavor, to strive, to prepare. Later my consciousness would expand sufficiently to learn that it is in the striving that enlightenment comes upon you like a ray of sunshine on a spring day.

I now openly profess that through our doors walk many Christs, many Buddhas. Spiritual consciousness is the destiny of all mankind. It is time for mankind to evolve into its next state of being.

Each individual must come to his own spiritual enlightenment at his own appointed time. Enlightenment cannot be bought or sold or loaned. It is not worn like a garment or awarded by another in recognition of effort.

Enlightenment is a state of being, a state of knowing, a state of consciousness. It is wisdom. As medical pioneer Jonas Salk, the inventor of the Salk polio vaccine, once remarked, "Wisdom is the fitness of the future."

Thanks to the School of Metaphysics, for everyone seeking wisdom, that future is now.

The vision is a place on Earth, open to anyone, where academic learning melds with spiritual disciplines, where arts and sciences are taught together, not as separate often clashing factions...Where anthropology teachers and students research the Akashic Record for Atlantean history. Where those desiring to serve as health practitioners are taught to be healers first. Where journalists are taught how to create the objective mind, counselors are taught the Universal Language of Mind, athletes are taught to master life force.

A college of the future. A place of learning for Spiritual Man.

Dreaming New Dreams

In 1993, I spent ten days in Chicago participating in the Parliament of the World's Religions.

One of the plenary sessions was given by Gerald Barney who is a founder and president of the Millennium Institute. Their work is concerned with problem solving on a world scale: population overgrowth, pollution, the worldwide increase of "haves" and the "have not's".

Following Barney's address to the gathering of hundreds, I attended one of the smaller sessions where people were invited to dialogue. One subject that arose, which was very enlightening to me, was what one attending journalist called "intentional communities." This is basically people having the intention of coming together and living together for a common purpose. The group began discussing how this might be one of the answers to the problems that we all face. I was intrigued.

I raised my hand to respond to a question Barney had posed, and opened my comment with "I live in one on these communities."

Immediately, everybody's attention was directed to me. It was like a magnet! It was shocking to me because I didn't expect it. I thought. "My God, this is profound."

My consciousness entered a new realm of realization because I realized most people have no idea what it is like to live as I do and so such a different "lifestyle" provokes keen interest. People want to know what motivates strangers to come together and live as family? What is it like when they do? And as a wise professor of abnormal psychology told a class years ago, "I know if I ask, you will say you are taking this class because you have a brother, sister, friend, roommate....who is a little strange.

But I want you to know that I know, you are here because you want to find out if you are a little strange."

We are curious because we want to understand.

The answers are not so far removed from most people's lives. For instance, we encourage our children to interact at young ages. We send them to grandma's for a week or let them stay at a friend's house overnight so they can begin to understand that family extends beyond what they have known. This prepares them for interaction with others in a school setting.

At some point during adolescence most children experience summer camp. Man's progressive movement of collective consciousness shines here for there are camps for everyone: those of the same religious faith, similar talents, the same disease, and interests ranging from sports to space. For many parents summer camps are a way to give their children something they want while freeing mom and dad for a couple weeks. In reality they are much more.

Camps are mind-altering experiences. They plant seeds of the power of common ideals. Where common ideals are realized friendship blossoms. Where friendship exists, understanding replaces hatred, the unknown becomes known. In the summer camps I mentor, young people discover their intuitive aptitude forging bonds within themselves and with others. It is more than building memories that will last a lifetime, these common experiences are the foundation for adult choices that make our future.

These eager, youthful minds learn what can be accomplished when people share a common vision. It is a preparatory step for the college experience. Camps fulfill the adolescence need to identify, to express, to be with your own kind. College fulfills the need to sustain individual integrity while interacting with others.

In the early '70's, the university experience expanded my world because it expanded my consciousness. College in those days was a privilege more than an expected extension of public education. Having come from a small community, the University of Missouri was the first time I had the opportunity to meet and live with people from other countries. What I learned from this experience has remained with me. I understood that beyond the physical trappings of looks, accents, cultures, people are the same. They have similar desires. They want to make a home, provide for their families, leave the world a different, better place. This is part of man's inner nature, it does not depend upon man-made territorial demarcations, it depends upon something beyond physical origins. The Universal Truth of this has been borne out again and again through my life

The dream of people living together, harmoniously, thrives among youth. It always has and it always will. At times the older ones would attempt to kill the dream, to spare the youth the pain of disillusionment. Stories of withholding blessings because of the choice of marriage partner or disinheritance for unapproved behavior still exist in much of the world.

For those of us in the United States the tide turned in the 1960's, that restless glimpse of the transitions to come. Beyond its lack of grace, stood universal principles of hope, love, peace. Spiritual endeavors approached in artificially induced stupors made the effort uncoordinated at best but it was effective, leaving its mark on each person and upon a nation of people. The legacy is a maturity of the adolescents of the '60's. Some like Peter Pan still fight growing up while others have become what they most feared: "the establishment." In our search for maturity it is as though the older generation recognizes the need for change and yet lacks the impetus to personally cause it. The failing of integration illustrates this. Forced integration intended to speed up cooperation between blacks and whites. Within a generation, those of both races wanting better and safer places to raise their children vacated cities to form communities in suburbia. For a long time my husband, a Master in economics and metaphysics, has advocated carving cities into communities no larger than 100,000. Beyond the material advantage lies what will cause it to work: the best communities are where people know each other.

The images, from the '60's, of passive resistance stimulating cruelty in those ill-equipped to respond to nonthreatening offenders haunts everyone who ever sees them. Clubs and water hoses turned on blacks in the South and college students in the Midwest eventually gave way to four dead in Ohio and we all grew up a little bit. Such passive resistance was encouraged by, if not directly stimulated by, events on a continent a world away – the uprising against British rule in India led by Mohandas Gandhi. The world became a much smaller place this century and we are finding out who we really are as a human race.

We have learned that pinning hope on adolescents who are moldable and adjustable, eager and idealistic, has caused most of the innovations in every culture. This is so for universally true reasons.

Adolescents actively seek the common ground. Unlike the infant child who finds the common need fulfilled in family, the adolescent desires commonality and so actively creates it. Ball teams and pep squads, music and pierced body parts, clothing and recreation, all take on an exaggerated sense of importance as the adolescent searches to identify "who am I". It is the essence of the class struggle, the rich and the poor, the haves and have nots, that still rules the world to its detriment rather than its exhaltation. This is adolescent thinking in the hands of physical adults. It is the desire-thinking characteristic of adolescence that gives us the impetus to leave the farm and migrate en masse to cities. All seeking a common dream. By living with all kinds of people we find out who we are, what we are made of and what we are capable of producing.

What will bring about maturity in consciousness, what will cause the global adolescence to give way to a worldwide adulthood is spirit-motivation. It is this kind of thinking operating in the world today that is fueling the greatest changes.

It is this kind of love for our fellowman that will bring us into Spiritual Renaissance.

We are rich in this consciousness in these United States. We have always been willing to help our neighbors. Who our neighbors are continues to change. Today's adoptions enable multicultural families to easily form. Such examples of mixed families, be it mixed races or religions, are in most family trees, perhaps even your own. The fact that in the United States we live together with people of all races, nationalities, backgrounds, cultures, and religions is a testament to the visionary intention that set this country into motion over 200 years ago.

The American dream – of opportunity and the freedom to respond to that opportunity – brings people to the United States. It is this common vision that bonds people beyond all physical differences. Even differences in language pale, those willingly and willfully coming to this country are eager to speak the language of the land for that is part of the American dream. After several generations, the dream tends to disappear as material wealth supercedes spiritual value. What is needed is *imagination.* We must stop reinventing, and learn to project our consciousness into the future, living in ways we have yet to live.

We need a new dream. The United States can be a melting pot of everyone on earth. It can mature into an example of the family of mankind, a microcosm, the world in minature. Based on their writings and actions, this was the hope of the founding fathers.

The College of Metaphysics, where my husband, son and I make our home, is giving this dream life. We share meals and chores, laughter and tears, with people of all ages, walks of life, religions, colors, sizes, and shapes. Most come for a year, some stay longer. They come to learn the secrets of the universe and to teach them. We do more than live together, we make a life together. From my vantage point I experience a continuous parade of souls coming and going, receiving and giving, maturing and serving. It is a wonder to behold. More and more I realize I am living the future of mankind. For me spiritual renaissance is happening every moment.

The vision is a place on Earth, open to anyone,

where academic learning melds with spiritual disciplines, where arts and sciences are taught together, not as separate often clashing factions. Where understanding form opens the mind to artistic mathematics and imaginative science. Where learning transcends physical limits - no longer a slave to unknown inspiration, artists learn to create at will. No longer a slave to what is defined by the five physical senses, scientists learn to directly perceive truth with the sixth sense.

A conservative liberal arts and sciences university whose curriculum is dedicated to accelerating the evolution of mankind. Where the concept and workings of Karma become the backbone of studies in law. Where the spiritual law that governs every physical law is taught.

A place of learning where faculty practice and teach principles that govern reasoning, intuition, and enlightenment. Where anthropology teachers and students research the Akashic Record for Atlantean history. Where those desiring to serve as health practitioners are taught to be healers first. Where journalists are taught how to create the objective mind, counselors are taught the Universal Language of Mind, athletes are taught to master life force.

A college of the future. A place of learning for Spiritual Man.

Since its inception in 1973, we have envisioned a campus in southern Missouri, where the School of Metaphysics started. In the country away from already established metro areas, land is plentiful for growth and expansion. It is also virgin, and so we can cooperate with nature in our design and building. We have always known the campus will center around a large pyramid, a scale version of the Great Pyramid of Giza, whose form naturally collects and disseminates energies that we will then receive and channel for productive uses. Around the pyramid will be geodesic domes in clusters of three that will house students and their teacher. This has been the dream from the beginning. It is the dream today.

In 1982, the first manifestation of the dream reached the material world with the purchase of over 700 acres of paradise in southwest Missouri just north of Branson. Since then the campus has doubled in size.

Rolling hills, mountain cliffs, riverbanks, wooded areas, natural springs, here you are in the presence of nature, creation and its Creator. We awaken to the bright chirps of cardinals and go to sleep to the tree frogs' lullaby. Deer and wild turkey have their times and seasons for daily treks across the campus. And for every tree cut and put to use, at least 10 new ones are planted. We share the land with life forms native to this area. It is a community in the fullest sense of the word. Meditations are rich here.

Although such community is not the reason the School of Metaphysics exists, community is nurtured in each individual and to the degree it takes root that inner communion shines forth in our relations with others. As one of the metaphysics lessons describes it:

> *"Friendship is the universal spiritual attraction uniting souls in bonds of Divine love. It can manifest itself in relationships between two or many people. Spirit is and was one. By the Law of Duality, Spirit became two, positive and negative. Then, by the Law of Infinity applied to the Law of Relativity, it becomes many. Now the one in the*

many is endeavoring to unite the many and make One. The efforts of the soul to unite many souls with a common ideal and purpose works through intelligence, will, and intuition, finding its greatest expression in friendship."

The words are timeless because they describe Universal principles that guide the evolution of our universe. This is the inner communion that shines forth becoming community.

If you'd asked me when I was in college where I'd be in twenty-five years I would not have described what has come to be. I didn't have the capacity to envision it then, that hint of prophecy has come along the way. What I did possess, and what everyone who dreams dreams has within them , is the undeniable *urge to know*.

It is that common urge that will illuminate our way as we build a new dream, together.

XII

The Spiritual Renaissance

Fulfillment

"What education is to the individual,
revelation is to the whole human race."

– Gotthold E. Lessing, German dramatist (1729-1781)

"The thing always happens that you really believe in;
and the belief in a thing makes it happen."

– Frank Lloyd Wright, American architect (1869-1959)

Spiritual Fulfillment

Can You Make it as a Spiritual Teacher?

Based upon an address given at the College of Metaphysics outdoor amphitheater during the annual SOM Camp Out, July, 1988..

Stop a moment and reread the title of this chapter. Now read it aloud. Hear your own voice. Let the words you speak echo in your mind.

Can you make it as a spiritual teacher?

Such a simple question. The answer may be profound, but what is more intriguing and revealing is how the question is posed.

Sometimes through habit we take words we use too lightly. Having awareness of this weakness, I have endeavored for years to strengthen my ears' capacity to attend to what my lips speak, and my lips reflect what is in my mind and heart.

Words we use, anytime, any place, convey who we are.

The words in this question – *Can you make it as a spiritual teacher?* – were chosen very carefully. When I am forming a lecture or sermon I begin with a title which reflects the message I want to impart. Years ago, I was preparing an address for teachers of the School of Metaphysics. I meditated on what my message to these leaders should be and I received, "Can you make it as a spiritual teacher?"

Contemplating the depth of this idea, I thought to myself, "How many times have I asked myself that question, and how many times have I answered it?" I looked around and I thought about my close friends and I wondered, "How often do they ask themselves this question?" I figured some ask it as much as I do, some occasionally, a few, rarely. It was fitting for a group of people invested in teaching spiritual concepts and practices to be asked this question.

That was just the beginning.

As I developed this idea, explored it inwardly, I began to realize there are several ways you could read this question. There are several ways that you can interpret it, each commanding a different meaning and thus influencing the answer. Let's examine four of these.

If you are the kind of person who read this question, "CAN you make it as a spiritual teacher?" then this is for you. CAN you make it as a spiritual teacher? To me that means "is there a possibility?" "Do you possess the ability to accomplish this ideal? I want to tell you how the CAN works.

I have the privilege and pleasure of knowing a young lady. She is a divine presence on the earth. She is so bright. She is intelligent, so quick, and she is very disciplined. I met her when she was about six years old. She wants to be like her mother, as all young girls do. A couple years ago I started watching something develop in her that I had not seen before.

Her mother directed a School of Metaphysics, volunteering many evenings to teach adults the universal laws of creation, and the young lady started wanting to be at the school. She wanted to be around people who are actively learning to live meditatively. Every chance she got, she would influence her mother into bringing her over to the school. She was attracted to wisdom, she enjoyed being around adults who were at once youthful and learning, experienced and knowing.

She was never a distraction to the adults around her. She knew how to pay attention at the level of her will power, and when she wanted to do something different she knew how to educate herself, entertain herself. One night the adults talked for a long time, and the young lady became bored and moved to one of the classrooms.

The next morning when I went into that room, I saw the traces the young lady had left behind. Evidence of the class she had taught the night before covered the blackboard. While I had been teaching in the other room, she held her own class.

I remember "pretending" to teach when I was her age and younger. Perhaps you also "played school." What we learned in that "school" does not matter. You might have pretended teaching how to be a bug collector, what in time would become an entomologist. Or maybe you taught drawing or nursing or fire fighting skills. These youthful memories are essential links to the reason your soul is here, for in the innocence of the very early years of physical life we find the open connections between the inner and outer minds. Here we find the essence of what will lead to spiritual fulfillment as life unfolds and physical years pass by.

There is an inner drive, an urge in each one of us to teach. If you haven't recognized it in your life yet, you will. You have taught by your example and your words, either with intention or mindlessly. This inner drive to give to another, to share what we know, is the reason why there is a physical desire in most people to have children. Most people are unconscious of this. Think about it. What do you do from the time you bring a child into the world? If you have not had children, imagine it; if you have children you will know. It starts with *teaching* the child simple survival skills: how to roll over, sit up, walk, talk, bathe, eat. From the moment of birth you are more than a physical parent, you are a teacher. And the motivation to be the best teacher you can comes from the overwhelming love pouring forth from you each time you see your child respond.

With each skill taught something miraculous happens in the mind of the parent. Your view of life and how to live it is shared in your thoughts, words, and actions. The first time our ten-month-old son lost his newly found footing and tumbled, he sat stunned, looking pleadingly to me for reassurance. I connected with him intuitively, assessed he was physically fine, and I giggled, clapping my hands and praising him. I shared how enjoyable movement was and he responded in like kind. When I reached out he immediately pushed himself up again and was on his way.

Attitude matters.

If you don't have children, there may be times in your job when someone new comes in and you must teach them what you know. You can do so with excitement because you are helping someone else to succeed, and with clarity because you understand the steps to accomplish your job, or you can do so resentfully, even fearfully. Attitude matters, no matter what age the student and the teacher.

At this stage in evolution, there is no way that you are going to escape teaching. Someone is always watching you, always listening to what you say, and hopefully finding inspiration.

For those who question, "CAN I make it as a spiritual teacher?" the first thing to admit is there is no question about CAN. You CAN teach, and you have opportunities to teach all the time. When you realize this, it becomes a matter of what kind of teacher are you? What subject are you going to teach, and how well are you going to teach it? CAN is not a possibility, it is a probability because you are a human being.

Your history, your individual history, this lifetime is important to you. Those memories of what you played as child, particularly games and roles played when alone, reveal your inner, soul's desire. How you interpreted that play is important to you now as an adult. It can mean the difference between happiness and depression, emptiness and fulfillment.

Your greater history which includes past understood experiences that comprise the soul, has earned you the right to pass on a great many things. These are what genius is made of. These understandings are in each of us. The ability no one taught us this lifetime. The talent we have that no one knows where it came from because it doesn't run in our family. It may be a propensity for athletics or playing an instrument, or it may demonstrate itself as natural leadership or kindness. By stilling the outer mind and looking inward, you become acquainted by the vast wealth within your soul. Your wealth is not money. Your wealth is not land. Your wealth is not really even in the number of people who hold you in high esteem. Your wealth is in how many of those understandings it takes to be compatible with your Creator.

The *Bhagavad Gita* tells the story of everyone. Krishna is comparable in character to the Lord God of the Christian *Bible*. When you understand the inner workings of consciousness you come to realize these Holy works are talking about something inside of us, not outside. Krishna and Lord God are both representative of the deepest part within us, a divine sense of oneness often called the I Am. The other character in the *Gita* is Arjuna, comparable to David of the *Old Testament*. Arjuna is learning to wield reasoning, thus he signifies reasoning man, the capacity we hold to consciously draw upon memory and imagination at will.

The entire *Gita* is an interchange between these two parts of self as symbolized by Krishna and Arjuna. Arjuna questions, Krishna responds with timeless wisdom. At one point Krishna speaks to Arjuna about the rewards of teaching:

> *"They who shalt teach this divine wisdom – the supreme mystery – to those who are my servants; and who practicing true devotion to Me, doeth instruct them in My service; they shalt truly come unto Me. Heed my words, Arjuna, there shall not be any among mankind who doeth Me a greater kindness than this teaching and spreading of the truth – nor shall there be anymore dear to me than these"*

You CAN teach. You do teach. It is a probability.

The second way this question can be posed is: Can YOU make it as a spiritual teacher?

Most children imagine what they want their parents to be like. This usually arises because our parents are never exactly the way we want them to be, nor do they do everything we want them to do. This is the way most of us started imagining a better world. The better world from the child's view is for parents to be different than they are. As we grow older we continue to imagine. What if a teacher or a friend were different? An employee, boss, community leader? Then maybe we begin to think beyond our immediate environment to what might make our country a better place to live, and even the world.

First we imagine all the different things we would eliminate – stealing, murder, crimes against our fellow man. Maybe we extend this thinking to attitudes we find destructive – hatred, prejudice, lying, jealousy. When we continue the train of thought eventually we begin to imagine what might replace these "negatives." We start discovering what it is to imagine. We envision brotherhood and what that might mean, neighbor helping neighbor, trust among people, honest concern for another's welfare. We imagine never feeling the need to lock our doors again. We can see mothers who know it is safe to let their youngsters play in a park across the street. We envision spiritual leadership in our governmental representatives. We can see people sitting side by side around the world, joined in ideal and purpose, committed to solving the challenges before humanity. It is an exciting use of human potential.

Can YOU make it as a spiritual teacher?

It depends a lot on what you are capable of imaging. Are you a positive thinker or are you a negative thinker? I am reminded of a quote from Sen. Robert Kennedy that I learned in my youth, *"Some people see things as they are and ask 'Why?' I dream of things that never were and ask 'Why not?'"*

When it comes to teaching somebody something, do you tell him why he should *not* do something, warning him of all the things that might happen if he ignores your advice? That's how some parents teach their children. So this is how those children learn to think; in negatives born from fear.

Or do you tell people the benefit of an action? When you do this...you can expect this to happen. Given the choice how would you like to be taught? Benefits or threats, desire or regret?

It is universally true that if you want someone else to be something, try being that yourself first. When you do, all kinds of doors open.

One of my personal experiences in answering can YOU make it as a spiritual teacher came when I was a first series student in the School of Metaphysics in Columbia, Missouri. I had been teaching a correspondence class for about five months and had fervently desired teaching a class for weeks. Being young in the lessons, I was not yet being considered for starting a class at the school. By the time the opportunity presented itself I was so happy and excited that I did not have time to be nervous. I did not have any time to be scared of what I might not know. I knew without doubt that I wanted to share with others what I had learned that had made such a difference in my life. I wanted to be a channel to make this study available to others.

I had been teaching these people for two weeks. I remember vividly it was Easter weekend. My director was away visiting her parents and I was filling in during her absence. I made myself useful, transcribing intuitive reports and hosting visitors. All of a sudden on Saturday afternoon SOM President Jerry Rothermel walked through the door. Practically the first thing he said to me was, "Are you ready to move?"

I knew that I had better close my mouth a second and let my thoughts settle because I was saying "yes" and "no" in rapid succession over and over in my head. I was reeling. I didn't want to say what I would not be willing to back up so I tried to be calm and asked, "Why?"

He said, "Well, I need somebody."

"Where?" I asked. My journalistic training was carrying me through, asking the important questions - who, what, when, where, why, and how - to get the facts.

"Wichita, Kansas." I had never been to Wichita, Kansas. The nearest I'd been to even thinking about it was *The Wizard of Oz*, so in my mind it was a wasteland. The idea of going to Wichita was not particularly appealing to me.

But I wanted more information so I could talk myself into this. I had been meditating daily for quite some time and I had learned how to listen to that inner voice. From the moment Dr. Jerry asked if I'd move, that inner voice was saying "go, go, go." However I also heard an outer voice, and that voice was getting louder with each question.

The volume increased for the next 36 hours, until it was driving me crazy. When I would be centered and calm I knew the answer for me was go. But I wasn't too calm. I would think about my cat and my possessions – I had a lease on a two bedroom apartment, filled with stuff. I would think about my boss, a lawyer, and the good paying job with all the freedom I wanted. I would think about my class that I had just started, the students were only on lesson two! I would think about my parents – my God! They knew I was in the school and they knew that I had even started teaching, but to think about calling them and saying, "Guess what, I'm moving to Wichita, Kansas. I'm going to direct a School of Metaphysics there," was a bit scary. I didn't know how they would respond. I was twenty-two, a college graduate, and on my own and I valued what my parents thought of me. My mind was cluttered.

By Sunday evening I welcomed our weekly healing class. Each week students gathered to project healing energies to those requesting it. We usually had eight to twelve requests and this evening the number was particularly high. I had loved healing class from the first time I was eligible to attend. I was there every week and I had become quite proficient in my attentiveness and my perception. This night it was as if I knew nothing of the mechanics of concentration. My attention was scattered and I could not keep my attention on the work at hand. It was maddening for I knew others depended upon me and I was failing them. I kept thinking about calling my parents, calling my landlord, calling my employer, so in disgust, after healing class was over I went upstairs and spent some time by myself. As I had learned to do when I had a problem, I meditated on it.

As had occurred a couple of times during meditation, I received an answer referring me to a Biblical verse. What I heard was "*Exodus 3:2*". Immediately upon coming back from meditation, I went to a *Bible* and opened it to the passage about Moses and the burning bush. Before Moses receives the ten commandments from God, he is a shepherd living out his days among the people he was separated from in his youth. Into this ease and bliss comes destiny.

> *"And the angel of the Lord appeared unto him in a flame of fire out of the midst of a bush: and he looked, and, behold, the bush burned with fire, and the bush was not consumed.*
>
> *And Moses said, 'I will now turn aside, and see this great sight, why the bush is not burnt.*
>
> *And when the Lord saw that he turned aside to see, God called unto him out the midst of the bush, and said, 'Moses, Moses.' And he said 'Here am I.'*

God goes on to instruct Moses to lead the Jews out of Egypt, where they are held in bondage by the Pharaoh.

"Moses said unto God, 'Who am I, that I should go unto Pharaoh, and that I should bring forth the children of Israel out of Egypt?'

And he said, 'Certainly I will be with thee; and this shall be a token unto thee, that I have sent thee: When thou hast brought forth the people out of Egypt, ye shall serve God upon this mountain.'

And Moses said unto God, 'Behold, when I come unto the children of Israel and shall say unto them, The God of your fathers hath sent me unto you: and they shall say to me, What is his name? What shall I say unto them?'

And God said unto Moses, 'I AM THAT I AM:' and he said, 'Thus shalt thou say unto the children of Israel, I AM hath sent me unto you.'"

Immediately I understood why I was reading this part of the *Bible*.

By now you have a grasp of what the "I Am" of scriptures might mean in each of us;– our divinity, the highest manifestation of Self, the Ego closest to our Spiritual Creator. We've discussed the concept of I Am in many different ways so you can readily understand that when I read that passage it was like the sky opening. Clouds rolled away. My thinking cleared. I had an idea of what this I Am is, and I was committed to knowing more about it. I wanted a relationship with my I Am. I did not want someone else's words. I did not want somebody else talking about God, I wanted a personal relationship with God. I wanted to know that God hears me and I hear him. I knew this meditation had brought the answer to my prayer. Not just clarity in a decision to move from one town to another, but more importantly confirmation of an inner spiritual movement that would deepen my personal commitment to soul progression and strengthen my inner drive toward enlightenment.

At that moment, I knew it was not the president of SOM who

was sending me to Wichita. All he was doing was giving me an opportunity in the physical from a need that I could respond to. I knew that it was my I Am sending me, and I knew that by going I would be that much closer to that I Am.

You have an I Am too.

Do you know where your I Am is sending you? Do you have a relationship with It, because It *is* you.

As Confucius counseled,

"The Master said, 'Look closely into his aims, observe the means by which he pursues them, discover what brings him content–and can the man's real worth remain hidden from you, can it remain hidden from you?'"

With the expanded awareness of your I Am, YOU can make it as a spiritual teacher.

The third way you can look at this sentence is "Can you MAKE it as a spiritual teacher?

Can you?

The beginnings of the School of Metaphysics are eclectic. Several people were directly involved in its physical formation. The school's first president would often say that he never wanted to teach. I always found this a contradiction because when I first met him he was an excellent speaker, intriguingly knowledgeable and quite persuasive. To learn that he had not imagined teaching was shocking to me.

I would think about where I might be if my college roommate had never insisted that I go to that first class in metaphysics with her. I would imagine where I might be, what I might be doing. I would probably live a comfortable upper, middle class life in the suburbs. I'd be pursuing a career which would define in large part my value. I'd most probably be married to someone I would have a hard time trusting owing to misunderstandings from my childhood. If we had children I'd do the best I could, but I would tire of them easily, often handing them to day care while I worked to pay others to raise my children. I'd resent my mother meddling in my affairs, and feel torn by what I believed others expected from me. I'd try to be a good person, probably volunteering to serve others in some way, but I would not be happy and would probably have a few health problems or possibly be on medication of some sort. I would not meditate for I would not know how. I would probably pray only when I was in trouble and then not feel worthy to even be listened to. Others would think I was a good employee, wife, mother, leader, team player. I would be, and only I would know how empty I felt inside. I would live the life I created, chasing what I had been told most assuredly would make my life meaningful, and sometimes wondering what I had done wrong that the meaning was inconsistent.

That is what I imagine, based on self knowledge of the first twenty two years of my life. How accurate a picture it is I will never, gratefully, know. But I've learned a lot about what creates lines of probability and I'm so very glad I learned how to create, to make, a meaningful existence.

A large part of what gives my life meaning is loving others, aiding them in some way to accomplish their dreams. The sense of sharing what I have found to be true has always been a part of me. When I was young and we played "school" I not only wanted to be the teacher, I wanted to be the principal because the principal knew all the students. I enjoyed teaching others to read, or listening to my peers' problems and giving them advice. Teaching has always been a desire even when I might be uncomfortable with it.

When I began wanting to teach metaphysics, both my desire and the discomfort became apparent. I wanted to teach because I wanted to make what I had learned available to others. But I had fears. The depth of them were brought to light when I received a Past Life Profile about four months into my metaphysics studies.

As is true with these intuitive reports, a *significant* incarnation was identified and described in detail. Briefly, this was a Mayan incarnation, where I was again female. At an early age, I had been chosen to be trained in a temple of religious worship for the people. The reporter described,

> "....*We see this one to have been greatly honored in this and to take great pride in this position; to be very enthusiastic and to attempt to project this enthusiasm to others. We see this to involve a certain disciplinary procedure which requires great attention being placed upon certain areas and we see this one to pursue this with great diligence and enthusiasm. We see the purpose set forth in this activity to be the enlightenment of other individuals and the building forth within self the complete enlightenment and unfoldment of the lower self to the higher.*
>
> *We see this one to pursue these studies, to reach a point where this one is able to disperse this information to other individuals. We see at this point this one to become quite distraught and upset within self, for this one has a great amount of insecurity that this one has not faced up til now. We see this one to view this passing on of information as a great responsibility and to be overly concerned with this one's doing this in a correct manner.*
>
> *Therefore after great inner turmoil and much time spent in arriving at a decision, we see this one to withdraw from these temple duties and withdraw from this study for this one feels the lack within Self to adequately demonstrate*

these qualities and project the proper information to others as this one would see to be in a perfect manner. We see this one to be very distraught over doing things in what would be considered a perfect way instead of doing things in a manner which is the best of her abilities.... (91475JW8)

The report goes on to describe the many years remaining in that life, years that were physically productive but in comparison to my early ones, spiritually delinquent. Now you can perhaps better understand the projected, without-metaphysics life scenario I painted.

Without any doubt I understood this woman in the profile. I knew her. I was not certain of the reality of reincarnation when I received this report, but I was very certain that what I received was about me, for me. The reality of my present life was relevant to this past life profile. I was again invested in spiritual ideals, rooted in discipline, that are "considered and used in every aspect of life." I knew teaching was part of my metaphysics studies, and having a sense of the immensity of the study, I knew I was scared of being able to teach it well to others. And yes, perfection was an important motivating force in my life then, either as something to strive for or to rebel against. For this reason alone, the past lifetime information was invaluable to me.

Yet, it would be the significance of this past lifetime to the present that would leave a stamp on my consciousness, changing my destiny forever.

"We see this one presently to also have a desire to reach out to others and to pass on to them the knowledge and experience this one has reached. And to do this in such a way as to always express with enthusiasm and a positive attitude to where these will respond and recognize the value of those things that this one seeks to give. We see this one

to have some degree of insecurity in doing this and this to relate primarily with the purpose this one has sought in choosing this lifetime and this time period.

We see this to be an extension of desire that has not been fulfilled in the past and the need at the present time to completely express during the present period.

We see this one to have formed a great deal of strength and independence from the past, and to still find the need to express self in this way, and to do this in such a way as to further the purpose and goals this one has set forth for self. Suggest to this one that there is no need this one feels insecure, for the finding of security in what this one presents is gained through experience and this one is in the process of forming this.

Suggest to this one to see self in the positive manner that this one projects to others, for through this and through the continuous application of those principles received, this one will form the security this one requires and will be able to share with others in the proper approach.

We see this one also to have error in attitude regarding the perfection of self in all activities. Suggest to this one that perfection is not required in experience upon the earth plane, but only the performing of the activity to the best of one's ability. Therefore, do not deny self the right to make errors, for errors can be valuable learning tools...."

The reality of what was being said moved through my being. I did more than hear and understand the words on an intellectual level, these were thoughts that aligned my consciousness. I was in touch with the reality of my inner self and I knew it. No doubt. No hesitation. Having been raised with a very strict definition of what is right and what is wrong, wrong had been unacceptable to me. I had never given myself freedom to evaluate the possible value of wrong although I had learned from mistakes in my life. Resolving these lines of thinking would last for years to come, but here, in this past life profile, I had a place to start.

My fear of others' misunderstanding did not go away when I heard this report, that would require years of experience as a teacher. What did start to crumble was the fear of not being perfect. Now I realized I had been chasing something that is not required for spiritual growth. The simplicity of how the report described the error in my attitude was incisive and freeing. I could now begin exploring what performing activity *to the best of my ability* meant.

I know what it is like to want to help others but fear that they will not accept what you have to offer. Every teacher is confronted with whatever fear of rejection their consciousness may harbor. Those who learn from it, go on to make great teachers. Those who don't eventually quit.

I have met many people who have never considered teaching. I have learned that just because you don't have a burning conscious desire to teach does not mean that the urge to teach is not within you. If you are like one of these you are like one of the founders of the School of Metaphysics. He did not want to teach either.

If you've always wanted to teach, you are more like me.

When I think about how teaching impacts the teacher, I am reminded of Chapter 10 of *Revelation* from the *Bible*. Beginning at verse eight:

> *"And the voice which I heard from heaven spake unto me again, and said, 'Go and take the little book which is open in the hand of the angel which standeth upon the sea and upon the earth.'*
>
> *And I went unto the angel, and said unto him, 'Give me the little book. And he said unto me, 'Take it, and eat it up;*

and it shall make thy belly bitter, but it shall be in thy mouth sweet as honey.'

And I took the little book out of the angel's hand, and ate it up; and it was in my mouth sweet as honey: and as soon as I had eaten it, my belly was bitter.

And he said unto me, 'Thou must prophesy again before many peoples, and nations, and tongues, and kings."

This passage gives us insight into our need to teach. Whether in metaphysics or in sports or in academics when you learn at an accelerated pace you quickly come to a point where you are full. In these days of internet and television it is called information overload. You absorb all you can hold. You come as far as you can, in order to go further you must make some room. One way to make some room is to give to others from the abundance that is yours. Fulfilling a desire to learn is sweet, and the responsibility for fulfilling that desire is to make learning available to others. Thus the great cycle of life continues.

After two decades of teaching applied metaphysics, I know that students reach this point of accountability. Those who accept responsibility, ascend to a new level of learning. It is dual in nature for you learn because you are teaching. You find out what you know and become aware of what you have yet to understand. Teaching fulfills the individual.

Just talking metaphysics is not enough. You can receive just so much intellectual information before your soul starts crying for some understanding of all that information you've collected in your brain. That is when it becomes sour in your stomach. If you don't want metaphysical indigestion, you will pass on what you are learning, as you are learning it. Then it can be made a part of you. The things that you make a part of you, the things that you really understand like the back of your hand are the things that you always have in your storehouse of wealth. It is an exciting concept that each one of us might just be that wealthy and might just be generous so we share.

Even though that reluctant teacher said he never wanted to teach, teach he did. And the ones he taught, taught. Those people in turn taught and somewhere in there I came along as did countless others as a recipient of teaching. I also became a giver of teaching, and in that way a lineage is created. One of the points of enlightenment that make the *Bible* outstanding is the symbolic lineage that produces a Christ. When you learn and teach it means much more to you to study Abraham, Isaac, Jacob, David, Solomon, all the others to Jesus who becomes the Christ.

I am proud to be part of a lineage of spiritual teachers, both in receiving teaching and in having a place to give it. Over the years I have witnessed how this ebb and flow affects humanity, one person at a time.

Can you MAKE IT as a spiritual teacher? When a potter makes a vase, he uses substance, usually clay. He invests his energy and makes a vase. When an employee makes money, he uses his skills as a service and this is in exchange for money. When you make love, you are experiencing a completeness because of what you are sharing with another person. You MAKE love.

To me making it means creating. Can you MAKE IT as a spiritual teacher? It all comes back to how much of a creator you are. We are told in all the world's holy books that we do have a Creator, a Maker. Someone, something, brought us into being. In the *Bible*, it says that we were not only brought into being, but we were made in the likeness and the image of that Creator, or God. This means that we were created with thought. Our real nature is spirit, not flesh. We also have similar attributes to our Maker, the like-ness. We can become like our Maker.

The volition, the free will that we were given when we were

brought into existence is one of our greatest assets. We have the freedom to teach. In the United States, we take so many of our freedoms in this country for granted. I meet people from parts of the world where they would not dare try to teach these ideas for fear of being arrested. Or worse, their lives being threatened. I am horrified of this existing in our world, and at the same time in awe that such fears never cross my mind when I think of telling someone about a new idea I have learned.

Think about it, when is the last time you thought, "I can't say that, I might get arrested! I don't dare, I might be killed!" This is alien thinking to one born and raised in a free society.

What *does* cross your mind? What will the neighbors think? It really is a living Hell to be a prisoner of your own making, your own creating. Living in a bondage of your own thoughts limits you. That is the travesty in our country at this time. You take for granted what you have long enough and you do lose all awareness of it. It might as well not exist anymore. Appreciate your freedom to teach. Embrace it! Run with it. Go as far as it can possibly take you.

All activity, collectively, at the School of Metaphysics we describe as teaching teachers. That is what we do. The reason why we do this, to whatever our capabilities, is because that is the only activity that is going to fulfill the ideal and purpose with which we were created.

The fourth way to view the question: Can you make it as a SPIRITUAL teacher?

When you are invested in metaphysics, the lives of the great masters becomes intriguing to you. Their lives offer inspiration and instruction in the quest for enlightenment. This is because these men, and women, were developing mastery. You know how they did it? Each great master developed mastery through teaching about spirituality. They did it by teaching what is beyond the physical, material plane of existence. They did it by teaching what causes the physical effects to be what they are.

The Buddhist teachings say, *"No man is born a Master."* This is true of the people who became great masters. They were not born that way either. They knew that they CAN. They knew about the I and they knew about the MAKING IT. They had their sights set on being a SPIRITUAL teacher and that is why they are remembered centuries after they walked the earth.

I look for commonalties between the great masters. In this way I can learn about the consciousness that is spiritual, and emulate it. One thing that is common with masterful people is that they leave their homes and families. Jesus did it. Gautama did it. Zarathustra did it. What does that mean? Does it mean to sacrifice? Does it mean you lose contact with those you love the most? I used to wonder and think perhaps it is true that those closest to you understand you the least. Then I learned something new.

One day I was teaching and found myself describing the difference between a house and a home. A house is shelter for the body. A home is shelter for the soul. A home is where you, the Real You, live. Wherever you go, you take you with you. If you are not at home with yourself, there will never be a home for you anywhere else.

In terms of family, I believe every Master knew something that I learned when I began to read the Akashic Records consciously. At our stage of evolution, there are very few people who you have not known before. I am not speaking of cursory knowledge, rather I am talking about familial relations, cousins, brothers, sisters, parents, business associates, people you have lived with at another time and another place. The theory of six degrees of separation describes what to these great masters of consciousness is family.

Family is not built on blood, it is built on a stream of consciousness that interconnects all humanity. People wonder how some can abuse their own children, such people lack an understanding of connectedness, they do not realize as they harm another they harm themselves. The capacity for a woman to give birth to a child or a male's sperm to produce a child does not imply wisdom or even knowledge of family. It is merely the physical capacity to reproduce the species. The power is in the attitude.

We now possess the capacity to develop the mental capacity to produce the next species: Spiritual, Intuitive Man. I think that the great masters knew that home is where you are and that family is humanity.

Another commonality between the Masters is facing ridicule. Great Masters were often put down, rejected for their ideas. Many were murdered, martyred, for them. In the records of their teachings it is clear this is because they were uncompromisingly truthful, direct and innovative. Masters are outstanding. Their vision is far-reaching. They see things differently than the average because they do not live in a world others create. They know answers others do not. Have you ever noticed how it kind of upsets you when somebody around you seemingly always knows the right answer? You come to a point where you wonder, "Can't I be right just once?" That's ego. That's your drive to understand so you can be right. Undisciplined it is also the seed in the weak to destroy someone else.

The Great Masters of history were innovative. They produced miracles. They accomplished what others did not. They understood what was beyond the comprehension of the norm. From feeding multitudes to healing the sick to drinking poison without ill effect, I think that "miracles" comes back to being able to produce "more." It does not matter what you are starting with, the miracle is just "more." For instance, more begins when you realize that there is *more* to you than a physical body. This means you recognize that you are a soul first, and you have a temporary physical body to use while in the material world. You are not a body with a soul that hopefully God will save.

Or you realize you ought to be doing something *more* with your life. A good friend once told me that as she lounged watching television on Sunday evening following a weekend intensive with teachers, which she led, this thought crossed her mind. She laughed as she heard it. When she told me, I laughed as well. We both knew she had done more with her life than most dream, and we both knew the question was a way to challenge.

The Great Masters demonstrated the wisdom of "more." They knew thought is cause, as above, so below. They were in the world, but not of it. They became that way through teaching.

Another commonality is all the Masters seemed to have a destiny at birth even if they did not act on it until later in life. Gautama waited for his Saturn return before he left his father's palace to pursue his spiritual destiny. Jesus began teaching immediately after his, at age 30. Gautama's birth and Jesus' birth foretell their destinies as great spiritual teachings.

I have had a destiny since birth and so have you. I describe that as my assignment for this lifetime. It is not an assignment that was given to me by somebody else. It was given by the inner part of me, my subconscious mind or soul, for the outer part of me to fulfill while walking this earth. Physical life has become the series of steps that reveal what my assignment is and how I can best fulfill it. That's been part of the joy of unlocking the doors to the inner levels. Attending to that little voice I spoke of earlier. It makes every moment in meditation worth it and every day of living meditatively a reward unlike any I have received or could even imagine gaining in the material world.

We each have an assignment in this life. Our peace of mind depends upon our acquaintance with and fulfillment of the sacred duty that is ours alone.

When we become serious about accelerating spiritual progression, the way we see ourselves and the world changes. We know this because the question changes from a hypothetical based on capacity to a determination based on desire. "Can you make it as a spiritual teacher?" evolves with you.

Now the question is *WILL you make it as a spiritual teacher?* Each person is the sole determining force in this. Individual desire is the insightful motivation, individual will power is the strength to accomplish the highest ideal.

When you are committed to being a spiritual teacher your mind is connected with the minds of the Great Ones the world has known. You are mind-full of spirit. Your thinking is constantly elevated to the causal point of existence. This brings forth mastery in you.

This is a benevolent mastery for it continually reaches out to help others in their quests. Such a one is willing to teach the spirit. One of the universal laws is the Law of Abundance, some call it a law of prosperity. Simply stated, it is "He who aids others to abundance will be abundant." This is the reality of Self Mastery, and the secret of fulfillment. Such is the hope of Spiritual Renaissance.

Benevolence, self-less service, is the quality that will distinguish the coming renaissance from any that have existed before. Every renaissance claims its geniuses, its masters of art or science or philosophy or government. These men and women progressed all of mankind because they pressed their genius to work for the common good.

In the coming Spiritual Renaissance we will see a generosity that will astound the world. The consciousness of the genius will be elevated to the common good and his work will assume a quality rarely seen upon the planet. The affect of many achieving this level of mastery will significantly influence the consciousness of every man, woman, and child.

The genius will evolve into the mystic and the world, within and without, will be forever changed.

The Dhammapada describes it eloquently.

"A man is not born to mastery.
A master is never proud.
He does not talk down to others.
Owning nothing, he misses nothing.

He is not afraid.
He does not tremble.
Nothing binds him.
He is infinitely creative.

So cut through
The strap and the thong and the rope.
Loosen the fastenings.
Unbolt the doors of sleep
and awake.

The master endures
Insult and ill treatment
Without reacting.
For his spirit is an army.
He is never angry.
He keeps his promises.
He never strays, he is determined.
This body is my last, he says!

Like water on the leaf of a lotus flower
Or a mustard seed on the point of a needle,
He does not cling.

For he has reached the end of sorrow
And has laid down his burden.
He looks deeply into things
And sees their nature.
He discriminates
And reaches the end of the way.

He does not linger
With those who have a home,
Nor with those who stray.
Wanting nothing,
He travels on alone.
He moves with love among the unloving,
With peace and detachment
Among the hungry and querulous.

Like a mustard seed from the point of a needle
Hatred has fallen from him,
And lust, hypocrisy and pride.
He wants nothing from this world
And nothing from the next.
He is free.
Desiring nothing, doubting nothing,
Beyond judgment and sorrow
And the pleasures of the senses,
He has moved beyond time.
He is pure and free.

How clear he is.
He is the moon.
He is serene.
He shines.

For he has traveled
Life after life,
The muddy and treacherous roads of illusion.

He does not tremble
Or grasp or hesitate.
He has found peace.

Calmly
He lets go of life,
Of home and pleasure and desire.
Nothing of man can hold him.
Nothing of gods can hold him.
Nothing in all creation can hold him.
Desire has left him,
Never to return.
Sorrow has left him,
Never to return.

He has come to the end of the way,
Over the river of his many lives
And his many deaths.
Beyond the sorrow of health,
Beyond the great joy of heaven,
By virtue of his purity.
He has come to the end of the way.

All that he had to do
He has done.
And now he has won."

Teaching requires a high level of giving. A sacrificing of self for the welfare of another. I think it is time to redefine what it means to bring a child into the world. It is time to consider that we are vessels for souls to enter, evolved souls who want to serve even before the body knows how to.

A Soul's Mentor

an essay first published in January 1999

The United States uses 90% of the world's supply of Ritalin, a stimulant that affects the central nervous system the way amphetamines do.

Use and production of ritalin is up by 700% since 1991. Seventy five percent of the drug goes to children.

Nearly 5 million children and adults are diagnosed with Attention Deficit Disorder (ADD).

Some experts say 10% of our kids have it.

If all took Ritalin, 1 in 6 boys ages 5-12 would use the drug.
(*USA Today,* Fall 1998, Lawrence H. Diller, author of *Running on Ritalin*)

Americans believe drug abuse - more than crime or the breakdown of home life - is the biggest danger facing children, according to a survey of 1,501 adults conducted by Harvard's School of Public Health and the University of Maryland Survey Research Center. (*USA Today*, Summer 1998)

Recently I was eating lunch with a student here at the College of Metaphysics while my son Hezekiah and his friend Briana were playing five feet away. Hezekiah, who is almost four years old, was moving his super balls from a basket into a box in order to transport them upstairs.

Every once in a while he would call Briana's name, compelling her to look and eventually inviting her participation.

After watching him for some time Bill said, "He never stops."

"Rarely," I replied, "he's quite something. So quick, so bright, so vital and vibrant."

I went on to tell Bill that if I was twenty years younger, without my metaphysical background, Hezekiah would probably join the increasing legions of bright but unruly kids being drugged by well-intentioned parents, teachers, and physicians within the next two years.

I would be like a growing number of mothers. I would have a profession that demanded my attention and that a good part of my identity depended upon. I would have stopped breast feeding by the second month, if tried it at all, partly so I could return to my job. My son would have been cared for, and in large part raised by someone else, whether a relative, friend, or employee paid out of the money I made while working elsewhere.

I would have believed I was doing the right thing. Providing the best for my child.

I would not know what to do to calm him. I would often find myself too tired to respond well to cries for attention, misinterpreting the plea for love and discipline as something else and thus failing to fulfill my child's needs. And my own.

At some point, as early as three, the caregiver might show concern for my son's disruptiveness, disobedience, or mere absent-mindedness. If I delayed I might find my child refused care or even schooling. I would seek a doctor's advice.

Being a good physician, he would tell me that once we start there is no stopping and two to three doses everyday are required. The drug does not heal. Ritalin is thought to increase chemicals in the brain and to simulate the inhibitory receptors producing the result of a stimulant drug's acting to increase inhibition. Nobody knows the long term affects but while drugged my child would be able to focus on what is at hand and learn.

Eventually I'd give in. Believing I was doing, if not the best for my child, at least what I had to do. His constant energy supply would be chemically altered through daily doses of socially acceptable and even fashionable drugs.

I would lose my son.

More importantly, he would lose himself.

Yes, he wouldn't be such a problem for others anymore. Not so demanding.

Nor so bright and inventive.

This is not just a hypothetical projection of what could have been in my life, it is the story of increasing numbers of parents I am meeting and counseling. Too often we, as a society, look for an easy way out. Pills are seen as an easy way out, just look at the shelves of every pharmacy section in your local market. It is a symptom of denial, stemming from a lack of self discipline. On the whole, Americans don't know how to discipline themselves toward positive, productive thinking that leads to health so they don't teach this wisdom to their children.

The greater problem we will face ten, twenty, forty years from now. Only then will we realize, individually and collectively, what we have caused by putting millions of human beings at age 4 or 6 or 8 on a type of "speed". The mental, emotional, and physical effects upon that child as he or she enters puberty or when he is 16 or 29 or 42 or 60 will be known only as time progresses.

This is just the physical perspective.

The real problem is once we get there it will be too late to change several generations of drug abuse, intentional drug addiction. We may never know the losses to individuals or society.

We must change.

Attitudinal changes are the hardest. Yet when children are involved mothers and fathers can and have often moved mountains.

When I identify the significant changes in my thinking that have produced the conditions in my life that have led me to be a parent, a role by the way that I did not visualize for myself from the time of puberty until I was 41 years old, I hope there is insight that can help others.

First realizing I am more than a body. Coming to terms with the difference between and separation of mind and body freed me to put the physical world in a more proper perspective. In time what had been important in my mind - steady relationships, financial security, being needed and valued - was replaced by a more deep-thinking, spiritually-centered, service-motivated consciousness. This led to the current conditions in my life, including a wonderful husband who is my life partner and our visionary lifestyle that enables my husband, son and I to live and work together. It also brings some wonderful people into our son's life. Many teachers, each with different areas of expertise to offer.

Second, taking my next step in understanding myself as a soul. The idea of a soul is something I was taught as a child, but it was lost in a turbulent adolescent because it was belief based rather than knowing based. Maturing my idea of soul, bringing it to the here and now rather than leaving it before and after birth, caused major shifts in how I see myself and others. This became very meaningful when I was pregnant. My husband and I communicated with the soul who became our son Hezekiah before he entered this life. By learning his soul needs we could prepare ourselves to respond to them.

Now, as he is growing, we can encourage his talents and teach the skills that will prepare him to meet his destiny. It frees me to learn and teach in ways foreign to how I was taught as a child. I can respond to Hezekiah's intense Michelangelo-scale illustrations of Moses and the Burning Bush which persisted every morning for three months then give way to a month of scientific invention including waterfalls made from suspending a ladle on a facet spout and tongs used as arm extenders to put superballs in places otherwise beyond his reach.

Third, learning that thought is cause and developing the will power to apply the knowledge. Concentration exercises were essential in this process, and are an important part of what my husband and I are teaching our son. The capacity to focus attention at will directed my creative energies and laid the foundation for reasoning skills to flourish. I have taught hundreds of adults the basics of how to use mind effectively - undivided attention, remembering, imagination, listening - and it is such a joy to be able to teach them to such a new soul. And quite a challenge for someone accustomed to the civilities of adulthood.

Advanced development in intuition is an enormous asset. Being able to connect with Hezekiah is essential in him knowing we love him and in teaching meaning behind actions. I have found my own creativity stretched and so in the midst of a "crying jag" I can connect with Hezekiah's soul, "crying" with him which quickly provokes giggles thus breaking the nonproductive train of thought so a more productive one can be introduced.

Fourth is acting upon a desire to aid others. Together my husband and I have almost fifty years of teaching experience. We teach metaphysics, understanding the universal laws and truths that govern creation and how to live in harmony with them. We both know it is the most fulfilling life anyone can hope to have.

I have met many people in my life who function under the mistaken belief that it is easier to teach children than adults. If that is so, we would not be drugging our brightest children in order to "control" them. We would be teaching them to become the geniuses they are meant to be.

Teaching requires a high level of giving. A sacrificing of self for the welfare of another. I think it is time to redefine what it means to bring a child into the world. It is time to consider that we are vessels for souls to enter, evolved souls who want to serve even before the body knows how to.

Hezekiah is such a soul. He is not attention deficit anymore than probably 99% of those diagnosed as such. There may be moments when his mom is attention deficit, from being tired or preoccupied thus her mind and body are not in the same place. Hezekiah knows it, every time. And he lets me know it too, which is becoming a great enrichment in my life for I am able to practice being here now in ways I totally missed before.

There's nothing wrong with Hezekiah's attention. Rather his attention is free, vital, lightning quick, and so very easy to arrest when the mind meeting his is focused and wizened.

I am dedicated to being such a focused, wise mind, for to me I am much more than my child's parent, I am a soul's mentor. That is the greatest any of us can ever hope to be.

XIII

The Spiritual Renaissance

Interconnectedness

"God frees our souls,
not from service, not from duty,
but into service and into duty,
and he who mistakes the purpose of his freedom
mistakes the character of his freedom.
He who thinks that he is being released from the work,
and not set free in order that he may accomplish that work,
mistakes the condition into which his soul
is invited to enter."

–Phillips Brooks, American Episcopalian bishop (1835-1893)

Spiritual Interconnectedness
A Higher Calling

In the religious teachings I was taught as a child, it is known as "The Calling".

It is no longer socially acceptable to publicly speak of it because it might mean you are too devout. Too inclined to the supernatural, the Godly. It might mean you have experienced something someone else hasn't, and they might be hurt, offended, or feel discriminated against. So you don't often hear it spoken of in the public arena, not in the '90's.

Yet if you listen you will hear the beckonings of the coming change. There are those who dare to speak the word. Gen. Colin Powell, a turn of the century Presidential candidate-in-waiting in the eyes of the American media, spoke of the Calling in his autobiography. He says he never heard the Calling for the ministry as his mother would have liked. But he found a Calling in becoming and being a disciplined and conscionable leader of men and women.

The Calling is the unmistakable and irresistible urge — Godly in origin and nature— toward thoughts and actions will serve for the good of all mankind.

It is destiny that is sacred.

It is what gives meaning to life.

It is what makes someone become a doctor, not for the financial security, but for the desire to see others well and without pain. And it is the response to the Calling to aid others that can elevate that doctor to become a healer.

It is what makes someone want to teach, not for a didactic power, but because nothing compares to seeing the light in a child's, or an adult's, eye when a new awareness is born or a new skill mastered. It is this joy in responding to the Calling by aiding others to abundance that makes a teacher wealthy.

It is what makes someone want to raise a child, not from lust or for ego gratification, but because they have so much love to give. It is the response to the Calling for the giving of love that brings them closer to their own Creator.

It is what makes someone want to hold public office, not for historical fame, but because they have a sense of the common good and a vision to embody it. It is the response to the Calling to lead that makes a statesman and philosopher for any age. The heart of the Calling is the mind of God and so the hands exist to serve our fellowman.

As William Shakespeare noted in *As You Like It*, there are many forms of service depending upon the motivation of the server.

> *"O good old man? how well in thee appears*
> *The constant service of the antique world,*
> *When service sweat for duty, not for meed!*
> *Thou art not for the fashion of these times,*
> *Where none will sweat but for promotion,*
> *And having that, do choke their service up*
> *Even with the having."*

Service is the act of giving with the intention of fulfilling the needs of another. Service can be expressed in many forms—an attendant to a bride or groom, a legislator considering the tenets to govern a nation, an older child watching over an infant, an adult tending to the health and well-being of an elderly relative, a group of people inventing, making, and distributing a product to make others' lives better, an aspirant communing with his Creator. Service does indeed come in many forms.

How do we make the service we give the best we have to offer? The 18th century English poet Samuel Johnson noted, *"It is our first duty to serve society, and after we have done that, we may attend wholly to the salvation of our own souls. A youthful passion for abstracted devotion should not be encouraged."* The needs of a child are many, thus he demands service from those upon whom he relies. The needs of the adult are few, thus he gives service to that which is more expanded than himself. This is the time when your own youthful passion can be harnessed and directed toward the fulfillment of your highest calling, your duty to your Creator and mankind. As the 19th century American philosopher Ralph Waldo Emerson observed, *"So nigh is grandeur to our dust, So near is God to man, When Duty whispers low, "thou must, The youth replies, "I can."* This is the greatest service into which we can bring ourselves — that giving, that action, that service which shines in its divine generosity.

The quality of service we are capable of giving depends upon our willingness to give freely — without hesitation or restriction or condition. To serve is to open the mind beyond any limitation; to receive your connectedness with all of creation and ultimately your maker. This is the true service into which we can all strive — a sacred service that warms the heart and enriches the soul of Self and all others — service which is the response to Duty.

The English poet William Wordsworth called *duty* the *"stern daughter of the voice of God."* And who of us has not at some time believed that duty is a hard taskmaster? Perhaps that sense of duty came at a young age, beckoning us to make our own way apart from the pack, the crowd, the group. And we, being innocently committed to an ideal whose import we were ill-equipped to communicate, found ourselves the object of peer's scorn. The blacksheep. The teacher's pet. The rebel. As we were steadfast and faithful in our response to duty, childish taunts hardened into slurs from those who refuse to understand, who are jealous, who would destroy someone else's dreams. Such people are found in every culture. And because of this, too many who hear God's voice at a young age grow deaf, abandoning the enlightenment responding to duty brings. Thus they do not teach their own children to listen.

Every person yearns. They constantly crave. Thus they seek what will ease the longing; that which will satisfy. Each person has equal opportunity for happiness or sorrow, prosperity or poverty, fulfillment or emptiness. Most have yet to realize what they yearn for is ethereal. Their time on earth is spent pursuing pleasures of the flesh -- pleasures that are transient, and that too often bring pain. The fame passes, the children leave home, the house deteriorates, the spouse dies. Eventually they come to realize what they want is the understanding that comes from aiding others, from passing on what they know, from creating a home, from loving.

As you heed your inner urge, your sense of duty, that *"voice of God,"* you trust in a higher power than any you have known before. Such communion with your Creator is beyond compare. Service becomes serving God and we come to understand what Jesus taught when he said, *"You cannot serve God and mammon."* By manifesting service in its most enlightened form we come to understand Krishna's counsel to Arjuna in the *Bhagavad Gita* to perform his duty and perform it well. We come to understand how to respect God and keep his commandments for as it is written in *Ecclesiastes: "this is the whole duty of man."*

How each man understands his duty dictates how he will fulfill it. Abraham Lincoln, the sixteenth president of the United States, knew well the importance of duty. He knew what it was like to be in the service of God: *"Let us have faith that right makes might, and in that faith, let us, to the end, dare to do our duty as we understand it."* Duty is a special form of service. Duty commands us to learn what is righteous and to live by the higher principles we come to understand. It demands that we change our limiting attachment and commune with the Source Who gave us life. Duty elevates service beyond the common and temporal toward the holiness of the exceptional and the transcendent.

In teaching metaphysics to others here in the West, I often find that people are attracted to this study not for its spiritual intent but because they want to use the knowledge for physical gain . They have physical desires that they want fulfilled. They want a job, a car, a romantic partner. And they learn how to acquire these desires. They are content, for a while.

Not long ago how to aid this type of student was the topic of discussion during a teacher's conference. A question arose concerning how to keep the mind focused on gleaning understandings from life experience, a truer sense of duty, without becoming enslaved by the senses. This was a challenge for the teachers as well as the aspirants they guided. My suggestion was to place the question "What will God have me do today?" on the mirror they use in the morning. Each day, the teachers were to read this question and spend their day going about answering it.

Albert Schweitzer once remarked, *"I don't know what your destiny will be, but one thing I know: the only ones among you who will be truly happy are those who have sought and found how to serve."* When you realize your Maker has a plan for you, you have the courage to rise above the throng. You can do what you must, regardless of physical age, race, status, or culture. When your mind is filled with thoughts directed toward your Creator you are no longer afraid of other's judgements. What might have deterred you previously, vanishes.

The Calling comes to every one, at some time, some place. When it comes, you know it with your entire being. You hear the *"voice of God"* everywhere, and your spirit is forever free.

As a result of mental and physical genetics, we are closer to our own sense of wholeness than we have ever been before, more mature in our capacity to reason, more open to our intuitive potential.

Rapid Spiritual Growth

first published in May, 1995

It is common for those of us in the Western world to mark spiritual evolution in linear time. Celebrations of birthdays, anniversaries, and even the birth of spiritual masters, like Jesus or Guatama or Mohammed, are signified by a date on the calendar. This is reflective of man's stage of development as a thinker, a creator. There is an opening of consciousness that is moving us beyond physical achievement into the realm of ethereal substance, the domain of meaning that is reflective of vertical time.

In a linear fashion, each birthday signifies physical growth often accompanied by privileges like operating a moving vehicle or casting a vote for governmental leadership. Each anniversary marks the passage of time shared by two people who love each other or invested by someone in his life's work. Beyond marking time, annual dates are a measure for experience in our world. How many people, places, events occur between the time a child is born and the time of his third birthday? How many circumstances populate the lives of a couple celebrating their fiftieth anniversary?

In an even deeper, vertical sense these special dates mark the growth and expansion of a person's consciousness; the development of intelligence, mastery of knowledge, level of responsibility, are not determined by the physical passing of time. Rather they are reflected in it.

The rapid growth witnessed by new parents in the first few years of life seems to decline after those first few years. By the end of the second decade physical maturity is for the most part complete and by the third decade growth becomes a chain reaction to the physical situations in our lives.

Every parent knows well the "I can't wait until...." excitement of youth. Do we lose that impulse for rapid growth, that inner urge that expresses as courageous curiosity or do we lose connection to it and thus our ability to fan the flame of spiritual purification?

I believe the impulse for rapid spiritual growth exists in every human being. I believe it is stronger today than it has ever been before. We are older souls, ripened through countless incarnations, wiser far beyond the physical years indicated in this lifetime. As a result of mental and physical genetics, we are closer to our own sense of wholeness than we have ever been before, more mature in our capacity to reason, more open to our intuitive potential.

When we look at children, others, ourselves, as physical beings only, we miss the impulse and blossoming of the real growth we are here to accomplish. Awareness of what we are here to give also passes us by.

The celebrations associated with rites of passage are more than personal achievements, they connect us with all of our kind, all of humankind. Birth, family, work, marriage, children, death are universal experiences for physical man. The realization of sharing experiences that your parents had before you, that your neighbor will have next year, that a stranger half way around the world is also having at this very moment, commands an opening of the mind. It nourishes your mind, quenching the thirst for understanding. This is what changes you.

Throughout the past 50 or so millennia the human species has refined and developed the capacity for reason. The rewards of this effort have been encoded and passed on to each successive generation, scientifically, physically in the genetic structure, spiritually, etherically in the mind pattern. Man's development of memory and imagination are unparalled in any other life form on this planet. Man is as Shakespeare noted half a millennia ago *"the paragon of animals."* The time is quickly arriving when this animal-man that we have become will evolve into what we describe as spiritual-man.

Individually we quicken our personal evolution by cultivating understanding in every form – cooperation, respect, love, freedom, responsibility, courage, persistence, loyalty, and so forth. Each day. No longer do we wait for a date to bring a reward or permission for reflection and prediction. Well-intentioned action becomes its own reward every moment, lending itself well to drawing upon the best from yesterday and dreaming the greatest for tomorrow.

Spiritual truth becomes much more than something to consider once a week on Holy day. Spiritual truth becomes the tenets by which you measure every thought and deed. When this is your reality you can call yourself Spiritual Man.

When 25th century man looks back at the years we are now living, I am certain that it is this transition in consciousness – animal-man sacrificing himself to Spiritual Man – that will be remembered and exalted. This time which we are now living will indeed be seen as the birth of a golden age, an age of planetary Enlightenment. An age of realizing what is truly of value.

And the beginning of embodying value, living it, as never before seen on Earth.

May peace be with you all ways.

About the Author

A teacher, wife, mother, futurist, counselor, minister, intuitive reporter, editor, artist, composer, singer, designer, poet, administrator, media consultant and producer, Barbara Condron lives what she teaches. She makes a home with her husband Daniel and their son Hezekiah on the campus of the College of Metaphysics, an ever-growing community of people dedicated to living Spiritual Renaissance.

Essays

Rapid Spiritual Growth, *Thresholds Quarterly*, Vol. 16, No. 1, February 1998

Uncommon Consciousness, *Thresholds Quarterly,* Vol. 14, No. 4, November 1996

Love of Truth, *Thresholds Quarterly*, Vol. 15., No. 3, August 1997.

World Karma, *Thresholds Quarterly,* Vol. 14., No. 3, August 1996.

More than an animal, *Thresholds Quarterly*, Vol. 16, No. 2, May 1998

A Different World, *Thresholds Quarterly,* Vol. 15, No. 2, May 1997

We All Pray to the Same God, Fall, 1997 editorial

A Soul's Mentor, *Wholistic Health & Healing Guide*, Vol. 8, No. 1, January 1999

Service, *Thresholds Quarterly,* Vol. 14, No. 1, February 1996

Highest Duty, *Thresholds Quarterly*, Vol. 13, No. 2, May 1995

Original addresses...

Spiritual Initiation: Gateways to Awareness, 1993, Parliament of the World's Religions

Can You Make it as a Spiritual Teacher, July 3, 1988, SOM annual Conference

The Revelation of God in Man, October 1992, National Teachers Conference

The Courage to Talk with God, 1989 General Assembly Interfaith Church of Metaphysics

When the Christ Returns, Will You Follow Him? SOM Annual Conference, July 1989

Pandora's Legacy to Man, July1990 SOM Annual Conference

Summoning a Nation, July 1991 SOM Annual Conference

Spiritual Initiation, America's Special Destiny seminar, 1986

A Life Worth Living, August, 1994, National Teachers Conference

*All are available on cassette tape

References

Translations of the world's Holy Works are widely available making for a rich experience for study and understanding. Here are some I recommend.

The Holy Bible
Comparing interpretations from the original Hebrew and Greek into English yields great insight. For years I used the *New American Bible* (Thomas Nelson publishers) for its extensive footnotes. Unfortunately these have been all but deleted in later published versions. This text, the *New International Version* and the King James text are good sources. Currently instructors at SOM use George Lamsa's translation in their classes. The Biblical stories retold here combine all of these.

The Dhammapada
My favorite is *Dhammapada: The Song of the Buddha* by Thomas Byron. Vintage Books (quoted on page 270). *The Buddhist Bible* by Dugan & Goddard is an excellent resource. EP Dutton & Co., publishers.

The Tao Te Ching
The version by Gia-Fi Feng and Jane English published in 1972 by Vintage Books.

The Bhagavad Gita
My choice is the first I read and studied: *Bhagavad Gita: Message of the Master* by Yogi Ramacharaka, published in 1930 by the Yogi Publication Society. Other excellent versions are interpreted by Eaknath Easwaryn and Swami Pabhavananda.

The Upanishads
Eaknath Easwaryn's interpretation published by Nilgiri Press.

Analects
Analects of Confucius by Arthus Waley, published in 1938 by Vintage Books.

Any book of quotations can put you in the company of the greatest thinkers the world has known. From John Bartlett's *Familiar Quotations* to newer, more global editions, these books offer food for thought.

Books worth your time

Complete Works of Shakespeare by G.B. Harrison. My old college text still serves me well. Published by Harcourt, Brace, & World in 1952

Benjamin Franklin, an autobiography. A pleasure to be in the company of wise ones. Vintage books, pub.

Myths & Legends of all Nations by Herbert Spencer Robinson & Knox Wilson. Eclectic.

Classical Mythology by Mark P. O. Morford & Robert J. Lenardon. Another ever-valuable college text. David McCay Co. pub.

Universal Myths by Alexander Eliot. The universal truths that bind us all. Meridian Books, pub.

Power of Myth (or any other title) by Joseph Campbell. Based on interviews with Bill Moyers, Campbell's command of world mythology is staggering and compelling.

Timetable of History by Bernard Grun. The outstanding events in ten categories since the beginning of recorded history. Simon & Schuster, pub.

Book of Virtues by William J. Bennett. One version of the Fisherman story is here, plus so many parables that spark insight and provoke thought. Simon & Schuster, pub.

Superconscious Meditation and *Dreams of the Soul: The Yogi Sutras of Patanjali* by Dr. Daniel R. Condron. The first describes human potential in astounding ways; the second, how to cultivate it. SOM Publishing.

Additional titles available from SOM Publishing include:

Superconscious Meditation
Kundalini & the Understanding of the Whole Mind
Dr. Daniel R. Condron ISBN 0944386-21-0 $13.00

First Opinion
Wholistic Health Care in the 21st Century
Dr. Barbara Condron ISBN 0944386-18-0 $15.00

The Dreamer's Dictionary
Dr. Barbara Condron ISBN 0944386-16-4 $15.00

The Work of the Soul
Dr. Barbara Condron, ed. ISBN 0944386-17-2 $13.00

Uncommon Knowledge
Past Life & Health Readings
Dr. Barbara Condron, ed. ISBN 0944386-19-9 $13.00

The Universal Language of Mind
The Book of Matthew Interpreted
Dr. Daniel R. Condron ISBN 0944386-15-6 $13.00

Permanent Healing
Dr. Daniel R. Condron ISBN 0944386-12-1 $13.00

Dreams of the Soul
The Yogi Sutras of Patanjali
Dr. Daniel R. Condron ISBN 0944386-11-3 $9.95

Kundalini Rising
Mastering Your Creative Energies
Dr. Barbara Condron ISBN 0944386-13-X $13.00

Going in Circles
Our Search for a Satisfying Relationship
Dr. Barbara Condron ISBN 0944386-00-8 $5.95

What Will I Do Tomorrow? Probing Depression
Dr. Barbara Condron ISBN 0944386-02-4 $4.95

soon to be released...
The Spiritual Power of Healing
The Reappearance of Atlantis & the Ermergence of Spiritual Man
Metaphysics: Education for the Third Millennium
The Mystic Child

To order write:

School of Metaphysics
World Headquarters
HCR 1, Box 15
Windyville, Missouri 65783
U.S.A.

Enclose a check or money order payable in U.S. funds to SOM with any order. Please include $4.00 for postage and handling of books, $8 for international orders.

A complete catalogue of all book titles, audio lectures and courses, and videos is available upon request.

Visit us on the Internet at *http://www.som.org*
e-mail: som@som.org

About the School of Metaphysics

We invite you to become a special part of our efforts to aid in enhancing and quickening the process of spiritual growth and mental evolution of the people of the world. The School of Metaphysics, a not-for-profit educational and service organization, has been in existence for more than two decades. During that time, we have taught tens of thousands directly through our course of study in applied metaphysics. We have elevated the awareness of millions through the many services we offer. If you would like to pursue the study of mind and the transformation of Self to a higher level of being and consciousness, you are invited to write to us at the School of Metaphysics National Headquarters in Windyville, Missouri 65783.

The heart of the School of Metaphysics is a three-tiered program of study. Lessons introduce you to the Universal Laws and Truths which guide spiritual and physical evolution. Consciousness is explored and developed through mental and spiritual disciplines which enhance your physical life and enrich your soul progression. We teach concentration, visualization (focused imagery), meditation, and control of life force and creative energies. As a student, you will develop an understanding of the purpose of life and your purpose for this lifetime.

Experts in the Universal Language of Mind, we teach how to remember and understand the inner communication received through dreams. We are the sponsors of the National Dream Hotline®, an annual educational service offered the last weekend in April. Study centers are located throughout the Midwestern United States. If there is not a center near you, you can receive the first series of lessons through correspondence with a teacher at our headquarters.

For those desiring spiritual renewal, weekends at our Moon Valley Ranch offer calmness and clarity. Each Spiritual Initiation Session's mentor gives thematic instruction and guidance which enriches the Spirit and changes lives. One weekend may center on transcendent meditation, another on creative genius, another on wholistic health or understanding your dreams. Please feel free to contact us about upcoming sessions.

The Universal Hour of Peace was initiated by the School of Metaphysics at noon Universal Time (GMT) on October 24, 1995 in conjunction with the 50th anniversary of the United Nations. We believe that peace on earth is an idea whose time has come. To realize this dream, we invite you to join with others throughout the world by dedicating your thoughts and actions to peace for one hour beginning at noon [UT] on the first of January each year. Living peaceably begins by thinking peacefully. We invite SOMA® members to convene Circles of Love in their cities during this hour. Please contact us about how you can participate.

There is the opportunity to aid in the growth and fulfillment of our work. Donations supporting the expansion of the School of Metaphysics' efforts are a valuable way for you to aid humanity. As a not-for-profit publishing house, SOM Publishing is dedicated to the continuing publication of research findings that promote peace, understanding and good will for all of Mankind. It is dependent upon the kindness and generosity of sponsors to do so. Authors donate their work and receive no royalties. We have many excellent manuscripts awaiting a benefactor.

One hundred percent of the donations made to the School of Metaphysics are used to expand our services. Donations are being received for Project Octagon, the first educational building on the College of Metaphysics campus. The land for the proposed campus is located in the beautiful Ozark Mountains of Missouri. This proposed multipurpose structure will include an auditorium, classrooms, library and study areas, a cafeteria, and potential living quarters for up to 100 people. We expect to finance this structure through corporate grants and personal endowments. Donations to the School of Metaphysics are tax-exempt under 501 (c) (3) of the Internal Revenue Code. We appreciate any contribution you are free to make. With the help of people like you, our dream of a place where anyone desiring Self awareness can receive wholistic education will become a reality.

We send you our Circle of Love.